SEO 2017

LEARN SEARCH ENGINE OPTIMIZATION
WITH SMART INTERNET MARKETING STRATEGIES

Expanded & Updated

Adam Clarke

Simple Effectiveness Publishing, Publisher.
Cover Design: Simple Effectiveness Publishing.
Production and Composition: Simple Effectiveness Publishing.

Adam Clarke has completed a certificate in the Google Analytics and Google AdWords Individual Qualification programs.

SEO 2017: Learn search engine optimization with smart internet marketing strategies.
Adam Clarke
Kindle ASIN B00NH0XZR0
Print ISBN-13: 978-1539151142
Print ISBN-10: 153915114X

TABLE OF CONTENTS.

1. Introduction to how Google works.
- Old-school methods that no longer work.
- Google updates and how to survive them.
- Authority, Trust & Relevance. The three powerful SEO strategies explained.
- How Google ranks sites now — Google's top-10 ranking factors revealed.
- How to stay ahead of Google's updates.

2. Keyword research. The most important step of SEO.
- Why is keyword research so important?
- What exactly is a keyword?
- How to generate a massive list of keywords.
- How to find keywords that will send traffic to your site.
- How to find keywords for easy rankings.

3. On page SEO. How to let Google know what your page is about.
- How to structure your site for easy and automatic SEO.
- How to make Google pick up the keywords you want.
- How to get more people clicking on your rankings in Google.
- Site load speed — Google magic dust.
- The usual suspects — sitemaps.xml and robots.txt.
- Duplicate content — canonical tags and other fun.
- Usability — the new SEO explained.
- Readability — SEO for the future.
- How to accelerate traffic and rankings with fresh content.

- How to target Featured Snippet rankings in Google's search results.

4. Link building. How to rank extremely high on Google.
- Why is link building so important?
- The dirty little secret no one wants to tell you about link building.
- How to acquire links and what to avoid in link building.
- Anchor text. What's all the fuss?
- Simple link building strategies.
- Advanced link building strategies.

5. Social media & SEO.
- Is social media so important for SEO?
- Google+ & SEO.
- Facebook & SEO.
- Twitter & SEO.
- Other social networks.
- Social media analytics.

6. Web analytics in a nutshell. How to measure your success.
- Why use Google Analytics?
- How to use Google Analytics.
- Acquisition.
- Organic Search report.
- Segments.
- Common web analytics terms explained.
- Other web analytics tools.

7. Troubleshooting common SEO problems & how to fix them.
- What to do when your site is not listed in Google at all.
- What to do when your business is not ranking for your own business name.
- What to do when your rankings have dropped off.

FREE SEO CHECKLIST PDF AVAILABLE AT THE END OF THIS BOOK

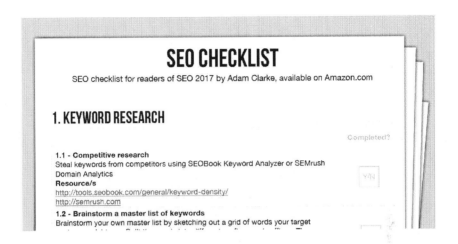

The free +50-point SEO 2017 - SEO Checklist PDF, covering exact steps to improve your website's ranking in Google, is available for readers at the end of this book. Instructions on downloading the SEO checklist PDF are available at the end of the book.

PREFACE TO THE UPDATED EDITION.

It didn't take long for this book to become a best-selling search engine optimization book after its original publication. The unexpected success of this book can only be attributed to its focus on making a powerful but difficult skillset easy to understand.

This book has been expanded and updated to cover how SEO works now and likely in the near future. All of the resources and tools have been updated and made relevant for 2017. It includes broader coverage of the basics, and filled with more techniques for advanced users. And due to requests by readers, it has been loaded with more helpful tools and resources so you can save time and get bigger results.

If you are a beginner, there is a small amount of technical information included in this book. If you really want to learn search engine optimization this cannot be avoided. We've made these areas as simple as possible, while providing additional tools and resources that will make it easy to speed up your journey to SEO mastery.

If you are an advanced SEO optimization professional, this book covers updated summaries of Google's latest updates, updated summaries of SEO marketing best practices to refresh your memory, solutions for common technical problems, and new tools and resources to sharpen your skillset—all written in an easy-to-read format, so refreshing your knowledge doesn't feel like a chore.

If you have requests for future updates, please contact me using my details at the end of this book and I'll be happy to take on board your suggestions.

INTRODUCTION.

So you've picked up *SEO 2017* and decided to learn search engine optimization. Congratulations! SEO marketing has changed my life and it can change yours.

Over 10 years ago, I achieved my first number one ranking in Google for my family's home business. The phone started ringing with new customers every day and I was hooked.

Since then, I have used search engine optimization to grow small family-owned businesses, sex toy stores, large international fashion brands and hotel chains. One thing never ceases to amaze me — the power of SEO as an Internet marketing tool for growing any business. I have grown small businesses into giant companies in just one or two years — simply from working the client's site up to the top position in Google.

Unfortunately, learning SEO is difficult, if not impossible, for most business owners, Internet marketers and even tech-heads.

I have a theory on why this is so...

Sifting through the amount of information flooding the Internet about SEO is overwhelming. In many cases, the advice published is outdated or misleading. And the constant updates by Google make it hard for SEO beginners and gurus alike to keep up with what works.

SEO can be simple and used by absolutely anyone to rank at the top of Google, grow their business and make money online. It's simply a matter of having up-to-date information on how Google works, using effective techniques and taking action.

Whether you're a complete SEO beginner or well-versed Internet marketing veteran, *SEO 2017* covers these areas and makes it as simple as possible to achieve rankings, traffic and sales.

Enjoy.

INTRODUCTION TO HOW GOOGLE WORKS.

You can feel like a dog chasing its own tail trying to figure out how Google works.

There are thousands of bloggers and journalists spreading volumes of information that simply isn't true. If you followed all the advice about SEO written on blogs, it's unlikely you would receive top listings in Google, and there's a risk you could damage your site performance and make it difficult to rank at all.

Let me tell you a secret about bloggers…

Articles about the latest SEO updates, techniques or tips are often written by interns, assistants or even ghostwriters. Their job is to write articles. The majority of blog posts about SEO are rarely written by experts or professionals with the day-to-day responsibility of growing site traffic and achieving top rankings in search engines.

Can you learn from someone who doesn't even know how to do it themselves?

You can't. This is why you have to take the advice spread by blog posts with a grain of salt.

Don't get me wrong. I love bloggers. There are bloggers out there who practice and blog about SEO, and do it well. But it has become increasingly difficult to sort the wheat from the chaff.

Fear not. This chapter will disperse common misconceptions about SEO, show you how to avoid falling into Google's bad books and reveal how to stay up-to-date with how Google ranks sites.

But first, to understand how Google works today, we must understand a little bit about Google's history.

OLD-SCHOOL METHODS THAT NO LONGER WORK.

Copyright ©1999 Google Inc.

In the early days of Google — over 15 years ago — Google started a smarter search engine and a better experience for navigating the World Wide Web. Google delivered on this promise by delivering relevant search engine results.

Internet users discovered they could simply type what they were looking for into Google — and BINGO — users would find what they needed in the top results, instead of having to dig through hundreds of pages. Google's user base grew fast.

It didn't take long for smart and entrepreneurially minded webmasters to catch on to sneaky little hacks for ranking high in Google.

Webmasters discovered by cramming many keywords into the page, they could get their site ranking high for almost any word or phrase. It quickly spiraled into a competition of who could jam the most keywords into the page. The page with the most repeated keywords won, and rose swiftly to the top of the search results.

Naturally, more and more spammers caught on and Google's promise as the "most relevant search engine" was challenged. Webmasters and spammers became more sophisticated and found tricky ways of repeating hundreds of keywords on the page and completely hiding them from human eyes.

All of a sudden, the unsuspecting Internet user looking for "holidays in Florida" would find themselves suddenly arriving at a website about Viagra Viagra Viagra!

How could Google keep its status as the most relevant search engine if people kept on spamming the results with gazillions of spammy pages, burying the relevant results at the bottom?

Enter the first Google update. Google released a widespread update in November 2003 codenamed Florida, effectively stopping spammers in their tracks. This update leveled the playing field by rendering keyword stuffing completely useless and restored balance to the force.

And so began the long history of Google updates — making it hard for spammers to game the system and making ranking in Google a little more complicated for everyone.

GOOGLE UPDATES AND HOW TO SURVIVE THEM.

Fast-forward 15 years and ranking in Google has become extremely competitive and considerably more complex.

Simply put, everybody wants to be in Google. Google is fighting to keep its search engine relevant and must constantly evolve to continue delivering relevant results to users.

This hasn't been without its challenges. Just like keyword stuffing, webmasters eventually clued onto another way of gaming the system by having the most anchor text pointing to the page.

If you are not familiar with this term, anchor text is the text contained in external links pointing to a page.

This created another loophole exploited by spammers. In many cases, well-meaning marketers and business owners used this tactic to achieve high rankings in the search results.

Along came a new Google update in 2012, this time called Penguin. Google's Penguin update punished sites with suspicious amounts of links with the same anchor text pointing to a page, by completely delisting sites from the search results. Many businesses that relied on search engine traffic lost all of their sales literally overnight, just because Google believed sites with hundreds of links containing just one phrase didn't acquire those links naturally. Google believed this was a solid indicator the site owner could be gaming the system.

If you find these changes alarming, don't. How to recover from these changes, or to prevent being penalized by new updates, is covered in later chapters. In the short history of Google's major updates, we can discover two powerful lessons for achieving top rankings in Google.

1. If you want to stay at the top of Google, never rely on one tactic.

2. Always ensure your search engine strategies rely on SEO best practices.

AUTHORITY, TRUST & RELEVANCE. THREE POWERFUL SEO STRATEGIES EXPLAINED.

Google has evolved considerably from its humble origins in 1993.

Eric Schmidt, former CEO of Google, once reported that Google considered over 200 factors to determine which sites rank higher in the results.

Today, Google has well over 200 factors. Google assesses how many links are pointing to your site, how trustworthy these linking sites are, how many social mentions your brand has, how relevant your page is, how old your site is, how fast your site loads... and the list goes on.

Does this mean it's impossible or difficult to get top rankings in Google?

Nope. In fact, you can have the advantage.

Google's algorithm is complex, but you don't have to be a rocket scientist to understand how it works. In fact, it can be ridiculously simple if you remember just three principles. With these three principles you can determine why one site ranks higher than another, or discover what you have to do to push your site higher than a competitor. These three principles summarize what Google are focusing on in their algorithm now, and are the most powerful strategies SEO professionals are using to their advantage to gain rankings.

The three key principles are: Trust, Authority and Relevance.

1. Trust.

Trust is at the very core of Google's major changes and updates the past several years. Google wants to keep poor-quality, untrustworthy sites out of the search results, and keep high-quality, legit sites at the top. If your site has high-quality content and backlinks from reputable sources, your site is more likely to be considered a trustworthy source, and more likely to rank higher in the search results.

2. Authority

Previously the most popular SEO strategy, authority is still powerful, but now best used in tandem with the other two principles. Authority is your site's overall strength in your market. Authority is almost a numbers game, for example: if your site has one thousand social media followers and backlinks, and your competitors only have fifty social media followers and backlinks, you're probably going to rank higher.

3. Relevance.

Google looks at the contextual relevance of a site and rewards relevant sites with higher rankings. This levels the playing field a bit, and might explain why a niche site or local business can often rank higher than a Wikipedia article. You can use this to your advantage by bulking out the content of your site with relevant content, and use the on-page SEO techniques described in later chapters to give Google a nudge to see that your site is relevant to your market. You can rank higher with less links by focusing on building links from relevant sites. Increasing relevance like this is a powerful strategy and can lead to high rankings in competitive areas.

HOW GOOGLE RANKS SITES NOW—GOOGLE'S TOP-10 RANKING FACTORS REVEALED.

You may have wondered if you can find out the exact factors Google uses in their algorithm.

Fortunately, there are a handful of industry leaders who have figured it out, and regularly publish their findings on the Internet. With these publications you can get a working knowledge of what factors Google uses to rank sites. These surveys are typically updated every second year, but these factors don't change often, so you can use them to your advantage by knowing which areas to focus on.

A short list of some of the strongest factors associated with high search rankings:

- Relevant keywords on the page.
- Keyword in internal links.
- User signals (click-through-rate, time-on-site, bounce-rate).
- Domain SEO visibility (how strong the domain is in terms of links and authority).
- Search volume of domain name.
- Total number of backlinks.
- Total number of referring domains (unique sites linking to your site).
- Google+ social media activity.
- Facebook social media activity.

If your competitors' have more of the above features than yours, then it's likely they will rank higher than you. If you have more of the above features than competitors, then it is likely you will rank higher than your competitors.

Combine this knowledge with an understanding of the recent Google updates covered in later sections, and you will know what it takes to achieve top rankings.

The above factors are from the Search Metrics Google Ranking Factors study released in 2016. The Search Metrics study is an in-depth look at the high-ranking factors in Google. If you want a deeper look, you can browse the full report by visiting the link below.

Search Metrics: Google Ranking Factors US
http://www.searchmetrics.com/knowledge-base/ranking-factors/

Another well-known authority on the SEO industry, called Moz (previously SEOmoz), release a survey every two years, combining survey data from world-leading SEOs, and a very detailed analysis of how Google functions today. Moz also publish this information for free.

Moz Ranking Factors Survey
https://moz.com/search-ranking-factors

HOW TO STAY AHEAD OF GOOGLE'S UPDATES.

Every now and then, Google releases a significant update to their algorithm, which can have a massive impact on businesses from any industry. To hone your SEO chops and make sure your site doesn't fall into Google's bad books, it's important to stay up-to-date with Google's updates as they are released.

Fortunately, almost every time a major update is released, those updates are reported on by the entire SEO community and often publicly discussed and confirmed by Google staff.

A long extended history of Google's updates would fill this entire book, but with the resources below, you can stay abreast of new Google updates as they are rolled out. This is essential knowledge for anyone practicing SEO, at a beginner or an advanced level.

You can even keep your ear to the ground with these sources and often be forewarned of future updates.

Google Updates by Search Engine Round Table
http://www.seroundtable.com/category/google-updates

Search Engine Round Table is one of the industry's leading blogs on SEO. At the page above, you can browse all of the latest articles on Google updates by a leading authority on the topic.

Moz Blog
https://moz.com/blog

The Moz blog is mentioned several times in this book and for good reason — it's pretty much the leading authority blog on all things SEO, and if there's an impending update Google have hinted at, you will catch wind of it here.

KEYWORD RESEARCH. THE MOST IMPORTANT STEP OF SEO.

WHY IS KEYWORD RESEARCH SO IMPORTANT?

Keyword research is the most important step of every SEO project for two reasons:

1. If you rank your site highly for the wrong keywords, you can end up spending lots of time and effort, only to discover the keywords you have targeted doesn't receive any traffic.

2. If you haven't investigated the competitiveness of your keywords, you can end up investing lots of time and effort into a particular keyword, only to find it is far too competitive to rank, even on the first page.

These two pitfalls are often the ultimate decider on how successful any SEO project is.

This chapter will cover how to avoid these pitfalls and how to find the best keywords. First, we must define what a keyword is.

WHAT EXACTLY IS A KEYWORD?

If you are an SEO newbie, you may be wondering — what is a keyword?

A keyword is any phrase you would like your site to rank for in Google's search results. A keyword can be a single word, or a keyword can also be a combination of words. If you are trying to target a single word, lookout! You will have your work cut out for you. Single word keywords are extremely competitive, and difficult to rank highly for in the search results.

Here's some different kinds of keywords:

Head-term keywords: keywords with one to two words, i.e. classic movies.

Long-tail keywords: keywords with three or more phrases, i.e. classic Akira Kurosawa movies.

Navigational keywords: keywords used to locate a particular brand or website. Examples would be Facebook, YouTube or Gmail.

Informational keywords: keywords used to discover on a particular topic. This includes keywords beginning with "how to…" or "what are the best..."

Transactional keywords: keywords entered into Google by customers wanting to complete a commercial action, i.e. buy jackets online.

In most cases, targeting head-term or navigational keywords for other brands is competitive and not worth the time or effort. Despite their high traffic numbers, they will generally not lead to any sales. On the other hand, long-tail, informational and transactional keywords are good keywords for most SEO projects. They will lead to more customers.

HOW TO GENERATE A MASSIVE LIST OF KEYWORDS.

There are many ways to skin a cat. The same is true for finding the right keywords.

Before you can find keywords with loads of traffic in Google, you must first develop a list of potential keywords relevant to your business.

Relevance is vital.

If you spend your time trying to cast too wide a net, you can end up targeting keywords irrelevant to your audience.

For example, if you are an online football jacket retailer in the United States, examples of relevant keywords might be:

Buy football jackets
Buy football jackets online
Online football jackets store USA

Irrelevant keywords might be:

Football jacket photos
How to make your own football jacket
Football jacket manufacturers
How to design a football jacket

You can see how the first pool of keywords are more relevant to the target audience of football jacket retailers, and the second pool of keywords are related but unlikely to lead to customers.

Keeping relevance in mind, you must develop a list of potential keyword combinations to use as a resource, so you can then go and uncover the best keywords with a decent amount of traffic each month in Google.

Following are some powerful strategies you can use to help with generating this list.

1. Steal keywords from competitors.

If you're feeling sneaky, you can let your competitors do the heavy lifting for you and snatch up keywords from their sites.

There are many tools out there created for this sole purpose. A simple and free tool is the SEOBook Keyword Analyzer. If you enter a page into this tool within seconds it will scrape a list of the keywords your competitor has optimized into their page. You can then use this to bulk out your keyword list.

SEOBook Keyword Analyzer
http://tools.seobook.com/general/keyword-density/

While the SEOBook Keyword Analyzer is a great, simple tool for revealing the keywords your competitors have optimized into the page, another powerful tool is SEMrush's Domain Analytics Organic Research Tool. This tool estimates the keywords that are sending the largest amount of traffic to your competitors' websites. The estimates are reasonably accurate and can be a valuable resource for bulking out your keyword list.

While SEMrush's insights are powerful, they do come at a cost. You can preview the first 10-keywords for free, but if you want more data its plans start at $69.95 per month for pro users.

SEMrush Domain Analytics
https://www.semrush.com

2. Brainstorm your own master list.

Assuming competitors have been thorough with their research isn't always the best strategy. By brainstorming combinations of keywords, you can generate a giant list of potential keywords.

To do this, sketch out a grid of words your target customer might use. Split the words into different prefixes and suffixes. Next up, combine them into one giant list using the free Mergewords tool. With this strategy you can quickly and easily build up a massive list of relevant keywords.

Mergewords

http://www.mergewords.com

Prefix
- buy
- where do I buy

Middle word
- NFL jerseys
- NFL uniforms
- NFL jackets

Suffixes
- online

Combined keywords
- NFL jerseys
- NFL jerseys online
- NFL uniforms
- NFL uniforms online
- NFL jackets
- NFL jackets online
- buy NFL jerseys
- buy NFL jerseys online
- buy NFL uniforms
- buy NFL uniforms online
- buy NFL jackets
- buy NFL jackets online
- where do I buy NFL jerseys
- where do I buy NFL jerseys online
- where do I buy NFL uniforms
- where do I buy NFL uniforms online
- where do I buy NFL jackets
- where do I buy NFL jackets online

- NFL jerseys
- NFL jerseys online
- NFL uniforms
- NFL uniforms online
- NFL jackets
- NFL jackets online

HOW TO FIND KEYWORDS THAT WILL SEND TRAFFIC TO YOUR SITE.

Now you have a list of keywords, you need to understand how much traffic these keywords receive in Google. Without search traffic data, you could end up targeting keywords with zero searches. Armed with the right knowledge, you can target keywords with hundreds or even thousands of potential visitors every month.

Unfortunately, in recent years Google has restricted access to the data behind Google's search box, leaving us with two options for finding keyword traffic data.

Firstly, if you have an AdWords campaign running with Google and are already spending a modest amount, then you're in the clear, you can access this info for free in their Google AdWords Keyword Planner tool. If this isn't you, the other option is to use a paid keyword research tool for a small monthly fee, such as keywordtool.io. As a result of Google making search data unavailable to free users, free keyword tools disappeared from the market, making paid research tools the only viable option for finding traffic data for keywords these days.

If you're on a tight budget, then you can sign up for a paid plan with one of the many paid keyword research tools on the market then ask for a refund after doing your research. It's not nice, but it's an option — either way, you need the traffic data behind your keywords otherwise you are running blind.

1. **Estimating keyword traffic data with Google's Keyword Planner.**

Google Adwords Keyword Planner
https://adwords.google.com/ KeywordPlanner/

As mentioned, to access all the juicy traffic data provided by the Google AdWords Keyword Planner tool, you need an active Adwords campaign running, and must be spending at least a modest amount of money regularly. If this is you, sign in, click on Tools in the top-menu, click on Keyword Planner' then click on "Get search volume data and trends", copy and paste your keywords into the box. Select your country, and then click the blue "Get search volume" button. When finished, you will have the exact amount of times each keyword was searched for in Google.

Mmm. Fresh data. This is just the kind of data we need.

Now we know which keywords receive more searches than others, and more importantly, we know which keywords receive no searches at all.

Keyword (by relevance)		Avg. monthly searches [?]	Competition [?]	Suggested bid [?]	Ad impr. share [?]	Add to plan
football jerseys	⌇	720	High	A$1.50	0%	»
football jerseys online	⌇	320	High	A$1.13	0%	»
football jackets	⌇	30	Medium	-	0%	»
where to buy football jerseys	⌇	10	Medium	A$2.12	0%	»

(Ad group ideas | **Keyword ideas**   ⌇   ⬇ Download   Add all (4))

1. **Estimating keyword traffic data with a paid research tool like Keyword Tool.**

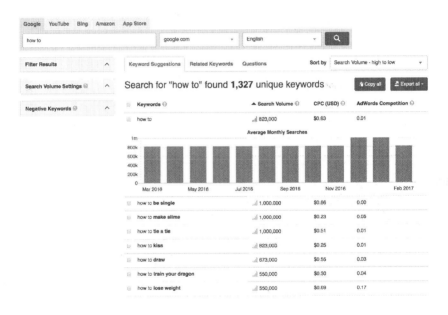

Keyword Tool
https://keywordtool.io

If you don't have an active AdWords campaign, or just simply want a research tool with a stronger SEO focus, then you can use a paid tool such as Keyword Tool. I like Keyword Tool for its ease of simplicity and relevant keyword suggestions, but you're not limited to this tool and there's many alternatives you can find with a couple of Google searches.

Using Keyword Tool as an example, once you have created an account, simply log in and enter your keyword ideas, take care to select your local search engine (e.g. google.com for USA, google.fr for France, etc) and select your local language, enter your keywords and download the juicy data. Now you can ensure you spend your time focusing on keywords that provide some traffic potential, opposed to chasing after keywords with no traffic and little opportunity for growing your business.

HOW TO FIND KEYWORDS FOR EASY RANKINGS.

Now you need to find out how competitive your desired keywords are. Armed with an understanding of how competitive your desired keywords are, you can discover keywords your site can realistically achieve rankings for in Google.

Let's say you are a second-hand bookseller and you want to target "book store online". It's unlikely you are going to beat Amazon and Barnes and Noble.

But, maybe there's a gem hiding in your list very few people are targeting — maybe something like "antique book stores online".

You have the advantage if your competitors haven't thought of targeting your keyword. You simply have to do better SEO than they are doing and you have a really good chance at beating their rankings.

You need a way to wash this list and separate the ridiculously competitive keywords from the easy keywords no one has thought of.

There are many schools of thought on how to do this. The most popular competitive research practices are listed below, with my thoughts on each.

1. Manually going through the list, looking at the rankings, and checking if low-quality pages are appearing in the top results.

This is good for a quick glance to see how competitive a market is. However, it is unreliable and you need to supplement it with real data.

2. Look at how many search engine results are coming up in Google for your keyword.

The amount of results is listed just below the search box after you type in your keyword. This tactic is common in cheap online courses teaching SEO, but completely unreliable. This is my least favorite strategy.

The reason? There may be a very low amount of competing pages for a particular keyword, but the sites ranked at the top of the results could be unbeatable.

3. Using the competition score from the Google AdWords Keyword Research tool.

Don't be tempted. This is a common tool, lauded on the Internet as an easy way to judge SEO competitiveness for keywords, and it just simply doesn't work!

The competition score included in the Google AdWords Keyword Research tool is intended for AdWords only. It is an indication of how many advertisers are competing for the particular keyword through paid advertising. Completely irrelevant for SEO.

4. Using a competitive analysis tool, such as Moz's Keyword Difficulty tool.

To get a realistic idea of your chances of ranking high for a particular keyword, you need to understand the strength of the pages in the top 10.

A great tool for this is Moz's Keyword Difficulty tool.

With Moz's Keyword Difficulty tool, you can simply enter your keyword into their tool, click "check difficulty", and then click "view serp analysis reports" and it will show vital stats for pages appearing in the top 10.

Of these stats, the most important are # root domains linking to the page, and # root domains linking to the root domain. These two stats tell you how many unique sites are pointing to the specific page ranking, and how many unique sites are linking to anywhere in the site in general.

Next up, if you enter your own website into Moz's Open Site Explorer tool, you can see these same stats for your site, and then know how many links you need to beat the competition.

Armed with this knowledge, you can hunt around to find easy keywords with weak competition, and set targets for how many links you need for a top listing.

You can use Moz's Difficulty Tool by signing up for a 30-day free trial. There are not many alternative keyword tools out there providing a decent level of accuracy in my experience, however, another tool I have found useful is Market Samurai, which offers similar reports to Moz.

Moz - Keyword Difficulty Tool
https://moz.com/researchtools/keyword-difficulty

Moz – Open Site Explorer
https://moz.com/researchtools/ose/

Market Samurai
http://www.marketsamurai.com/

When you have finished reading the book, you can work through the keyword research points in the free SEO checklist included at the end of the book, with a step-by-step approach.

ON-PAGE SEO. HOW TO LET GOOGLE KNOW WHAT YOUR PAGE IS ABOUT.

On-page SEO is the process of ensuring that your site is readable to search engines. Learning correct on-page SEO is not only important in ensuring Google picks up the keywords you want, but it is an opportunity to achieve easy wins and improve your website's overall performance.

On-page SEO includes the following considerations:

1. Making sure site content is visible to search engines.
2. Making sure your site is not blocking search engines.
3. Making sure search engines pick up the keywords you want.

Most on-page SEO you can do yourself, if you have a basic level of experience dealing with sites.

If you are not technically inclined, please note there are technical sections of this chapter. You should still read these so you understand what has to be done to achieve rankings in Google, you can easily hire a web designer or web developer to implement the SEO techniques in this chapter, after you know what it takes to achieve top rankings.

HOW TO STRUCTURE YOUR SITE FOR EASY AND AUTOMATIC SEO.

These best practices will ensure your site is structured for better recognition by Google and other search engines.

1. Search engine friendly URLs.

Have you ever visited a web page and the URL looked like something like this:

http://www.examplesite.com/~articlepage21/post-entry321.asp?q=3

What a mess!

These kinds of URLs are a quick way to confuse search engines and site visitors. Clean URLs are more logical, user friendly and search engine friendly.

Here is an example of a clean URL:

http://www.examplesite.com/football-jerseys

Much better.

Take a quick look at Google's search engine results. You will see a very large portion of sites in the top 10 have clean and readable URLs like the above example. And by a very large portion… I mean the vast majority.

Most site content management systems have search engine friendly URLs built into the site. It is often a matter of simply enabling the option in your site settings. If your site doesn't have search engine friendly URLs, it's time for a friendly chat with your web developer to fix this up.

2. Internal navigation

There is no limit on how to structure the navigation of your site. This can be a blessing or a curse.

Some people force visitors to watch an animation or intro before they can even access the site. In the process, some sites make it harder for visitors and more confusing for search engines to pick up the content on the site.

Other sites keep it simple by having a menu running along the top of the site or running down the left-hand side of the browser window. This has pretty much become an industry standard for most sites.

By following this standard, you make it significantly easier for visitors and search engines to understand your site. If you intend to break this convention, you must understand it is likely you will make it harder for search engines to pick up all of the pages on your site.

As a general rule, making it easier for users makes it easier for Google.

Above all else, your web site navigation must be made of real text links — not images.

If your main site navigation is currently made up of images, slap your web designer and change them to text now! If you do not have the main navigation featured in text, your internal pages will almost be invisible to Google and other search engines.

For an additional SEO boost, include links to pages you want visible to search engines and visitors on the home page.

By placing links specifically on the home page, Google's search engine spider can come along to your site and quickly understand which pages on your site are important and worth including in the search results.

HOW TO MAKE GOOGLE PICK UP THE KEYWORDS YOU WANT.

There are many misconceptions being circulated about what to do, and what not to do, when it comes to optimizing keywords into your page.

Some bloggers are going so far as telling their readers to not put keywords in the content of targeted pages at all. These bloggers — I'm not naming names — do have the best intentions and have really taken worry about Google's spam detection to the next level.

But it is complete madness.

Not having keywords on your page it makes it almost impossible for Google to match your page with the keyword you want to rank for. If Google completely devalued having keywords on the page, Google would be a crappy search engine.

Think about it. If you search for "Ford Mustang 65 Auto Parts" and arrive on pages without those words on the page at all, it's extremely unlikely you have found what you're looking for.

Google needs to see the keywords on your page, and these keywords must be visible to your users. The easy approach is to either create content around your keyword, or naturally weave your keyword into the page. I'm not saying your page should look like the following example.

"Welcome to the NFL jersey store. Here we have NFL jerseys galore, with a wide range of NFL jerseys including women's NFL jerseys, men's NFL jerseys and children's NFL jerseys and much, much more."

This approach may have worked 10 years ago, but not now. The keyword should appear naturally in your page. Any attempts to go bonkers with your keywords will look horrible and may set off spam filters in search engines. Use your keyword naturally throughout the content. Repeating your keyword a couple of times is more than enough.

It's really that simple.

Next up, you need to ensure you have a handful of LSI keywords on your page. LSI stands for Latent Semantic Indexing. Don't be discouraged by the technical term, LSI keywords is an SEO term for related phrases. Google believes a page is more naturally written, and has a higher tendency to be good quality and relevant, if it also includes relevant and related keywords to your main phrase.

To successfully optimize a page, you need to have your main keywords and related keywords in the page. Find two or three related keywords to your main keyword, and repeat these in the page two or three times each. Ubersuggest is a great tool for finding keywords Google considers related to your main keywords — it does this by pulling suggestions from Google's auto-suggest box. Use Ubersuggest and your keyword research to determine a list of the most related keywords.

Ubersuggest – Free
http://ubersuggest.io/

Areas you can weave keywords into the page include:
-        Meta description and meta title tags

- Navigation anchor text
- Navigation anchor title tags
- Headings (h1, h2, h3, and h4 tags)
- Content text
- Bolded and italicized text
- Internal links in content
- Image filename, image alt tag and image title tag
- Video filename, video title

HOW TO GET MORE PEOPLE CLICKING ON YOUR RANKINGS IN GOOGLE.

Meta tags have been widely misunderstood as mysterious pieces of code SEO professionals mess around with, and the secret to attaining top rankings. This couldn't be further from the truth.

The function of meta tags is really quite simple. Meta tags are bits of code on your site controlling how your site appears in Google.

If you don't fill out your meta tags, Google will automatically use text from your site to create your search listing. This is exactly what you don't want Google to do, otherwise it can end up looking like gibberish! Fill out these tags correctly, and you can increase the number of people clicking to your site from the search engine results.

Below is an example of the meta tag code.

<title>Paul's NFL Jerseys</title>

```
<meta description="Buy NFL jerseys online. Wide range
of colors and sizes."/>
<meta name="robots" content="noodp, noydir"/>
```

Below is an example of how a page with the above meta tag should appear as a search engine result in Google:

Paul's NFL Jerseys
Buy Paul's NFL jerseys online. Wide range of colors and sizes.
http://www.yoursite.com/

Pretty simple, huh?

The title tag has a character limit of roughly 70 characters in Google. Use any more than 70 characters and it is likely Google will truncate your title tag in the search engine results.

The meta description tag has a character limit of roughly 155 characters. Just like the title tag, Google will shorten your listing if it has any more than 155 characters in the tag.

The last meta robots tag indicates to Google you want to control how your listing appears in the search results. It's good to include this, otherwise Google may ignore your tags and instead use those listed on other directories such as the Open Directory Project and the Yahoo Directory.

To change these tags on your site you have three options:

1. Use the software your site is built on. Most content management systems have the option to change these tags. If it doesn't, you may need to install a plugin to change these tags.

2. Speak with your web designer or web developer to manually change your Meta tags for you.

3. If you are a tech-savvy person and are familiar with HTML, you can change these tags in the code yourself.

SITE LOAD SPEED—GOOGLE MAGIC DUST.

How fast (or slow) your site loads is another factor Google takes into account when deciding how it should rank your pages in the search results.

A very well-known Google employee, Matt Cutts, publicly admitted fast load speed is a positive ranking factor.

If your site is as slow as a dead snail, then it is likely your site is not living up to its potential in the search engines. If your site load time is average, improving the load speed is an opportunity for an easy SEO boost.

Not only is load speed a contributing factor to achieving top rankings in Google, extensive industry reports have shown for each second shaved off a site, there is an average increase of 7% to the site conversion rate. In other words, the faster your site loads, the more chance you have of people completing a sale or filling out an inquiry form. Clearly this is not an aspect of your site to be overlooked.

Fortunately, there are a handful of tools that make it easy to improve your load speed.

1. Google Page Speed Insights
https://developers.google.com/speed/pagespeed/insights

Google's great free tool, Page Speed Insights, will give you a page load score out of 100. You can see how well your load speed compares to other sites. You can also see how well your site loads on mobile and desktop. Scores closer to 100 are near perfect.

After running a test on your site, the tool will give you a list of high priority, medium priority and low priority areas for improvement. You can forward these on to your developer to speed up your site, or if you are a bit of a tech-head, you can have a crack at fixing these up yourself.

2. Pingdom Tools
http://tools.pingdom.com/

Pingdom Tools is great for an overview of how long your site takes to load in different areas of the world, and for a quick breakdown of files and resources that are slowing your site down.

After the test is completed, if you scroll down you will see a list of the files each visitor has to download each time they visit your site. If you discover files that can be decreased in size, you can improve your site load speed.

Easy targets for improvements are large images. If you have any images over 200kb, these can usually be optimized and shrunk down to a fraction of the size without any loss in quality. Take a note of these files, send them to your web developer or web designer, and ask them to compress the files to a smaller file size.

THE USUAL SUSPECTS—SITEMAPS.XML AND ROBOTS.TXT

Sitemaps.xml

Search engines automatically look for a special file on each site called the sitemaps.xml file. Having this file on your site is a must for making it easy for search engines to discover pages on your site. Sitemaps are essentially a giant map to all of the pages on your site. Fortunately, creating this file and getting it on to your site is a straightforward process.

Most CMS systems have a sitemaps file automatically generated. This includes systems like Wordpress, Magento, Shopify. If this is not the case on your site, you may need to install a plugin or use the free XML Sitemaps Generator tool. The XML Sitemaps Generator will automatically create a sitemaps.xml file for you.

XML Sitemaps Generator
http://www.xml-sitemaps.com

Next ask your web developer or web designer to upload it into the main directory of your site, or do it yourself if you have FTP access. Once uploaded, the file should be publicly accessible with an address like the below example:

http://www.yoursite.com/sitemaps.xml

Once you have done this, you should submit your sitemap to the Google Search Console account for your site.

If you do not have a Google Search Console account, the below article by Google gives simple instructions for web developers or web designers to set this up.

Add and verify a site to Google Search Console
http://support.google.com/webmasters/bin/answer.py?
hl=en&answer=34592

Login to your account and click on your site. Under "site configuration" click "sitemaps", and in the textbox, enter the full address to your site.

Robots.txt

Another must-have for every site is a robots.txt file. This should sit in the same place as your sitemaps.xml file. The address to this file should look the same as the example below:

http://www.yoursite.com/robots.txt

The robots.txt file is a simple file that exists so you can tell the areas of your site you *don't* want Google to list in the search engine results.

There is no real boost from having a robots.txt file on your site. It is essential you check to ensure you don't have a robots.txt file blocking areas of your site you want search engines to find.

The robots.txt file is just a plain text document, its contents should look something like below:

robots.txt good example

User-agent: *
Disallow: /admin
User-agent: *
Disallow: /logs

If you want your site to tell search engines to not crawl your site, it should look like the next example. If you *do not* want your entire site blocked, you must make sure it does *not* look like the example below. It is always a good idea to double check it is not set up this way, just to be safe.

robots.txt - blocking the entire site

User-agent: *
Disallow: /

The forward slash in this example tells search engines their software should not visit the home directory.

To create your robots.txt file, simply create a plain text document with Notepad if you are on Windows, or Textedit if you are on Mac OS. Make sure the file is saved as a plain text document, and use the "robots.txt good example" as an indication on how it should look. Take care to list any directories you do not want search engines to visit, such as internal folders for staff, admin areas, CMS back-end areas, and so on.

If there aren't any areas you would like to block, you can skip your robots.txt file altogether, but just double check you don't have one blocking important areas of the site like the above example.

DUPLICATE CONTENT—CANONICAL TAGS AND OTHER FUN.

In later chapters I will describe how Google Panda penalizes sites with duplicate content. Unfortunately, many site content management systems will sometimes automatically create multiple versions of one page.

For example, let's say your site has a product page on socket wrenches, but because of the system your site is built on, the exact same page can be accessed from multiple URLs from different areas of your site:

http://www.yoursite.com/products.aspx?=23213
http://www.yoursite.com/socket-wrenches
http://www.yoursite.com/tool-kits/socket-wrenches

In the search engine's eyes this is confusing as hell and multiple versions of the page are considered duplicate content.

To account for this, you should always ensure a special tag is placed on every page in your site, called the rel canonical tag.

The rel canonical tag indicates the original version of a web page to search engines. By telling Google the page you consider to be the "true" version of the page into the tag, you can indicate which page you want listed in the search results.

Choose the URL providing the most sense to users and the best SEO benefit, this should usually be the URL that reads like plain English.

Using the earlier socket wrenches example, with the tag below, Google would be more likely to display the best version of the page in the search engine results.

```
<link rel="canonical
" href="http://www.yoursite.com/socket-wrenches
"/>
```

As a general rule, include this tag on every page on your site, shortly before the </head> tag in the code.

USABILITY—THE NEW SEO EXPLAINED.

As mentioned in the first chapter, the trust and relevancy of sites has become increasingly important for Google. Market share for mobile and tablet Internet users skyrocketed to over 29% in 2015 — to keep search a good experience for all users, Google has started to give preference to sites providing a good user experience for users on all devices. Usability has taken an increased importance in the SEO industry as a result, as SEO pundits found you can get an advantage by making your site easy to use.

For example, let's say a mobile user is searching for late night pizza delivery in Los Angeles. One local business has a site with a large amount of backlinks but no special support for mobile users, it's difficult for the user to navigate around the site because it doesn't automatically fit to the screen, and the navigation text is small and hard to use on a touch screen.

Another competing local business has low amounts of backlinks, but good support for mobile users. Its design fits perfectly to the screen and has special navigation for mobile users, making it easy to get around.

In many cases, the second site will rank higher than the first, for mobile users. This is just one example of how usability can have a significant impact on your rankings.

While a term like usability can understandably seem a little vague, let's look at practical steps to improve your usability and the SEO strength of your site.

1. Make your site accessible for all devices.

Make your site accessible and easy for all users: desktop, mobile and tablet. The simple way to do this is to make sure your site is responsive, which means it automatically resizes across all devices and has mobile-friendly navigation for mobile users. Mobile support is covered in more detail in Bonus Chapter 2 in the Mobile SEO Update section, but you can enter your site into the below tool to quickly see if Google registers your site as mobile friendly.

Mobile friendly Test
https://www.google.com/webmasters/tools/mobile-friendly/

2. Increase your content quality.

Gone are the days of hiring a bunch of writers in India to bulk out the content on your site. It needs to be proofread and edited, and the more "sticky" you make your content, the better results you will get. If you provide compelling content, users will spend more time on your site and are less likely to bounce back to the search results. Users will also be much more likely to share your content. Google will see this and give your rankings a boost.

3. Use clean code in your site.

There's a surprisingly high amount of sites with dodgy code, difficult for both search engines and Internet browsers to read. If there are HTML code errors in your site, which means, if it hasn't been coded according to industry best practices, it's possible your design will break when your site is viewed on different browsers, or even worse, confuse search engines when they come along and look at your site. Run your site through the below tool and ask your web developer to fix any errors.

Web standards validator
https://validator.w3.org/

4. Take it easy on the popups and advertisements.

Sites with spammy and aggressive ads are often ranked poorly in the search results. The SEO gurus have reached no consensus on the amount of ads leading to a penalty from Google, so use your common sense. Ensure advertisements don't overshadow your content and occupy the majority of screen real estate.

5. Improve the overall 'operability' of your site.

Does your site have slow web hosting, or a bunch of broken links and images? Simple technical oversights like these contribute to a poor user experience.

Make sure your site is with a reliable web hosting company and doesn't go down in peak traffic. Even better, make sure your site is hosted on a server in your local city, and this will make it faster for local users.

Next up, chase up any 404-errors with your web developer. 404 errors are errors indicating users are clicking on links in your site and being sent to an empty page. It contributes to a poor user experience in Google's eyes. Fortunately, these errors are easy fixed.

You can find 404 errors on your site by logging into your Google Search Console account, clicking on your site, then clicking on "Crawl" and "Crawl Errors". Here you will find a list of 404 errors. If you click on the error and then click "Linked From" you can find the pages with the broken links. Fix these yourself, or discuss with your web developer.

Google Search Console
https://www.google.com/webmasters/tools/

If you want external tools to speed up improving your site's usability, I have found these two resources helpful:

BrowserStack - Free to try, plans start at $29 per month.
https://www.browserstack.com

BrowserStack allows you to test your site on over +700 different browsers at once. You can preview how your site works on tablets, mobile devices, and all the different browsers such as Chrome, Firefox, Safari, Internet Explorer, and so on. It's helpful for making sure it displays correctly across many different devices.

Try My UI - Free to try, additional test results start at $35.
http://www.trymyui.com

Try My UI provides videos, audio narration, surveys of users going through your site, and reports on any difficulties they uncover. Usability tests are good for larger projects requiring objective feedback from normal users. The first test result is free, making Try My UI a good usability test provider to start with.

READABILITY—SEO FOR THE FUTURE.

One of the strongest ranking factors has been flying under the radar, overlooked by many SEO professionals in their optimization checklists, leaving a golden opportunity for those that know about it. I'm talking about readability.

Google have been outspoken about readability as an important consideration for webmasters. Google's SEO spam king himself, Matt Cutts, has gone on to say that poorly researched and misspelled content will rank poorly, and clarity should be your focus. And by readability, this means not just avoiding spelling mistakes, but making your content readable for the widest possible audience, with simple language and sentence structures.

Flesch readability has since surfaced in the Searchmetrics' Google ranking factors report, showing a high correlation between high ranking sites and easy to read content. The Searchmetrics rankings report discovered that sites appearing in the top-10 showing an average Flesch reading score of 76.00—content that is fairly easy to read for 13-15 year old students and up.

It makes sense readability is a concern for Google. By encouraging search results to have content readable to a wide audience, Google maximise their advertising revenues. If Google were to encourage complicated results that mostly appeal to a smaller demographic, such as post-graduates, it would lower Google's general appeal and their market share.

You can achieve an on-page SEO boost, while also increasing your user engagement, by making your content readable to a wide audience. Run your content through a Flesch readability test. It will look at your word and sentence usage, and give you a score on how readable it is. Scores between 90-100 are easily understood by an 11 year old student, 60-70 easily understood by 13 to 15 year old students, and 0-30 best understood by University graduates. You can use the free tool below, and should aim for a readability score between 60-100. To improve your score, edit your content to use fewer words per sentence, and use words with a smaller number of syllables.

Readability Score
https://readable.io/

HOW TO ACCELERATE TRAFFIC AND RANKINGS WITH FRESH CONTENT.

The most overlooked, but powerful, on-page SEO strategy is adding more unique, fresh content to your site. If you consistently add new pages to your site, you are going to receive more traffic. In fact, not only can you increase your traffic, you can receive an *exponential* traffic increase as you publish more content.

It's a no-brainer when you think about it. This is why blogs, publishing and news-type sites consistently get good results in search engines. More content means more rankings, more visitors, and more sales. Let's look at getting started with improving your traffic by adding fresh content.

1. Post new content on a regular schedule.

If you are going to add new content to your site, you need to decide on a schedule and stick to it. This might seem obvious, but you would be surprised at the large number of businesses that talk about starting a blog and never get around to it. It's the businesses with a regular roster of adding content to their site that see regular increases in search rankings, increases in overall search engine performance, and a growing loyal audience. Without a dedicated roster or schedule, it will never get done.

If you don't have the capacity to create content yourself, or a budget to hire a full-time marketing assistant to create content, try hiring a ghostwriter.

Good quality writers can be sourced between $25-$75 USD per article and you can regularly churn out fresh content to your heart's content. Popular services can put you in touch with talented writers, such as Textbroker or the Problogger job board.

Textbroker
https://www.textbroker.com

Problogger Job Board
http://jobs.problogger.net

2. Leverage your social media accounts.

It almost goes without saying, but you should be leveraging social media to drive traffic to new posts or pages added to your site.

Whenever you post new content, post it across all of your social media accounts. Then post it again in a couple of days and you will expose your content to a different segment of fans. You'll increase your social activity and as a result get higher rankings.

3. Link up your site to blog aggregators.

Blog directories are an easy opportunity for high-quality backlinks, available for anyone running a blog. A handful of large authority blog directories accept site submissions and syndicate content—an opportunity to build up referral traffic. Simply ensure you have a base level of content to start, and then submit your site. A link to your blog can be approved within a week or two.

Here's a handful of high-quality blog directories accepting submissions:

http://www.alltop.com
http://www.blogarama.com
http://blogs.botw.org
http://portal.eatonweb.com/

HOW TO TARGET FEATURED SNIPPET RANKINGS IN GOOGLE'S SEARCH RESULTS

Ever searched in Google and saw your answer featured in a giant ranking sitting just above the search results? These large search results are called "featured snippets" and can send a mind blowing amount of traffic if you're clever enough to achieve one of these types of rankings. While achieving a featured snippet can be difficult, there's a couple of techniques for achieving one of these rankings.

Before I jump into the techniques, are you still not sure what I'm talking about? Quickly Google a couple of questions and look for the giant search result that answers your question at the top of the search results, you can't miss it—it's about three times bigger than a regular search result. Here's some example searches that usually deliver a featured snippet in the results, "how to get started in real estate", "how to increase your blog traffic", and so on...

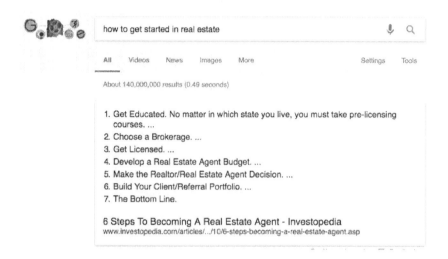

Featured snippets can be a tricky because there is no special code or tag you can use for these according to Google, quite simply, your answer needs to provide a great answer for your audience, or at least Google needs to see it that way. Fortunately for us, some clever SEO's have figured out some general techniques and criteria for targeting these sexy rankings.

1. Your desired ranking must be for a question type keyword. Searches that aren't phrased as a question generally won't trigger a featured snippet, so better to focus on question related keywords.
2. Your page must be performing okay generally. You don't necessarily need to be ranking in the top position, but if you're ranking on page 2 or page 3 of the then it's unlikely you'll achieve the featured snippet ranking, if this is the case, first focus on ranking higher. If you're already ranking around positions 1-4, then you have a much greater chance of being featured.
3. Your answer should be clear and concise. It almost goes without saying, well written and clear answers have a much greater chance of being featured then poorly written answers.
4. Provide more valuable information than a simple and direct answer. If your answer has numbered lists, rich media such as images and videos, and is generally more helpful than an obvious answer to the question, then you have a greater chance of being featured.
5. Include a Q&A or how to section on your site. Increase content in a question and answer format and you increase your odds of being featured for several pages.

Want to read up further on featured snippets? Eric Enge from Stone Temple Consulting provided a great write up on his studies and techniques ranking for featured snippets.

How to Get Featured Snippets For Your Site
http://searchengineland.com/get-featured-snippets-site-224959

~

That sums it up for the on-page SEO chapter.

If you have a small business, the technical factors mentioned earlier in this chapter are what will make the difference — such as ensuring your site has the right keywords and is accessible for all users.

If you are doing SEO for a large company and need a large amount of traffic, regularly publishing new content and ensuring structural areas of your site are setup correctly are what will make the difference — such as regularly posting new blog posts, ensuring you have sitemaps working correctly, and no duplicate content or 404 errors.

What's most important is you act. On-page SEO is often the easiest part of SEO. The power is in your hands to fix these areas in your site. Remember that small tweaks can lead to big results. Put these methods to practice and start improving your rankings.

Just like the keyword research steps, for readers who want to put the theory into practice, all on page optimization tips from this chapter are included in the SEO checklist. I do recommend finishing the book before downloading the checklist and the on page SEO steps, so you are familiar with the theory behind the practical steps.

LINK BUILDING. HOW TO RANK EXTREMELY HIGH ON GOOGLE.

WHY IS LINK BUILDING SO IMPORTANT?

The previous chapter described how to make your site visible to search engines and how to optimize keywords by using on page SEO. If you want to see your rankings improve by leaps and bounds, then your site needs links.

You may have wondered what makes link building so important, especially when there are so many factors Google use to rank sites.

The truth is, links are such a strong factor, it is unlikely you will rank high for a keyword if you are competing against sites with more backlinks.

When you think about it, links are the currency of the web. Each time a page links to another, it is a vote for the value of the page being linked to. If a page provides massive value to Internet users, it stands to reason it will be linked to from other sites. This is why links are such a strong factor in Google's algorithm.

Link building is the key to ranking your site high in the search engine results.

THE DIRTY LITTLE SECRET NO ONE WANTS TO TELL YOU ABOUT LINK BUILDING.

There are a lot of opinions circulating the Internet about the best kind of links to build to your site. So much so, they often escalate into heated discussions.

What is the best link? A link from a government site or from a high trafficked blog? Is it better to get a link from a highly relevant site or from a site with a lot of social media activity?

The dirty secret no-one wants to tell you about link building is *there is no single best kind of link.*

If this weren't the case, Google wouldn't work. Everyone would go out and find a way to spam their way to the top of the rankings very quickly. Having thousands of one type of link pointing to a page is suspicious and a clear sign the site owner is gaming the system.

That said, as a rule, you should try to build links on authoritative, relevant and high-quality sites. High-quality, relevant links are much stronger than links from low-quality, unrelated sites.

HOW TO ACQUIRE LINKS AND WHAT TO AVOID IN LINK BUILDING.

There are many stories floating around about business owners being slammed by Google for no good reason. Don't let the horror stories mislead you.

In most cases, what really happened is the webmaster was doing something clearly suspicious or outdated, like building thousands of links to their site from link directories, and then their rankings suddenly dropped off from Google's top-10 search results.

If you don't exhibit overly spammy behavior in your link building, as a general rule you will be OK.

These best practices will ensure you acquire links correctly and don't break Google's terms of service:

1. Acquire links naturally and evenly over time. Your links should be attained consistently and organically.

In fact, Google has made its approach with assessing link acquisition in relation to time public knowledge. Patent US20050071741 outlines how Google analyzes the age of links and the rate they are acquired and then uses this information to calculate the search results.

If you don't fancy reading up on patents in your spare time, then just remember to gradually build up your links over time, so Google sees that your website is acquiring links organically. Don't go out and buy one thousand links pointing to your site overnight or you're sure to set off a red flag in Google's system and get into its bad books.

2. As a rule, don't purchase links. Buying links with the intention of boosting your rankings is against Google's terms of service and you risk being penalized. These kinds of links may work, but are generally not worth the potential damage, unless you are confident you know what you are doing.

3. Forget about link-swapping or link-trading schemes. These are completely obvious to Google, and either no longer work or may harm your site. This goes against common knowledge, but I've achieved countless number one rankings for ridiculously competitive keywords without ever swapping links. Link-swapping is extremely time-consuming and completely unnecessary. Get by without it.

4. Don't spam message boards, article sites or blog comments with crappy content. This might work temporarily, but strategies such as these are outdated very quickly.

5. There are paid networks out there offering to build new links to your site for a low monthly fee each month. Never use them. These networks are against Google's terms of service and using them is a quick way to ensure you find yourself in hot water with Google.

ANCHOR TEXT. WHAT'S ALL THE FUSS?

There has been some controversy around anchor text, as touched on in a previous chapter. Anchor text is the text contained in a link. Anchor text *was* one of the strongest factors for achieving top rankings.
If you had one thousand links to your site with "NFL football jerseys" as the link text, and competitors only had a handful of links with the same anchor text, it was likely you would rank number one. That is, until Google's Penguin update effectively put an end for SEOs using "exact match" anchor text as their strategy. Now it is just simply too risky.

Not only is it no longer as effective as it once was, building hundreds of "exact match" links to a site actually can prevent it from ranking for that keyword.

So then, you might wonder, what is the best way to build up anchor text?

It should be natural.

It is OK to have your targeted keyword in your anchor text, but it should not be the only keyword or the main keyword in all of your links, and there should be a mix of related keywords.

If you think about it, this is a pattern all legitimate sites naturally attract. It defies logic that a quality site would automatically be linked with the exact same text throughout the entire World Wide Web.

Look over the below examples to see a bad anchor text profile compared to a natural anchor text profile:

Bad anchor text – external links
http://www.examplefootballbrand.com/football-jerseys.html
NFL football jerseys - 200 links

Good anchor text
http://www.examplefootballbrand.com/football-jerseys.html
examplefootballbrand - 50 links
NFL football jersey store - 10 links
NFL football jerseys - 5 links
http://www.example.com - 25 links
football jersey store - 5 links
football jerseys online - 5 links
football jacket store - 15 links
click here - 7 links
website - 15 links

The above good anchor text example illustrates the natural way sites accumulate links over time. Your target keyword should not be the most linked phrase to the page.

You can learn a lot by looking at the search engine results ranking in Google, enter high-ranking sites into Open Site Explorer, and looking at their anchor text. You'll notice almost every top-ranking page has natural anchor text, like the good example above.

Track your link-building efforts and keep them in a spreadsheet. This way you can monitor your anchor text and make sure it fits in with best practices.

Open Site Explorer
https://moz.com/researchtools/ose/

SIMPLE LINK BUILDING STRATEGIES.

The link building strategies below will help you build up quality links pointing to your site, and give Google a nudge to rank your site higher.

Directory links.

Directory links are a tried and true form of link building that received some flack in recent years. This is due to Google penalizing spammers who built ridiculous amounts of low-quality directory links to their site.

Directory links shouldn't be overlooked. In fact, directory links should be the first place to start with any link building project. There's a solid amount of high-quality business directories where you can get powerful and strong backlinks built with a minimum of effort.

But just to be safe, your directory links should not make up much more than 10-20% of your total links. They must also be relevant and quality sites, i.e. not sites with web addresses like seolinksdirectory.com or freelinksdirectory.com. Sites like these just smell of spam! Before building a link on a directory, ask yourself, "Does this look like a legitimate and trustworthy website?'" If the answer is no, then move on and focus on legitimate, quality sites only.

To find relevant directories, use the below search terms in Google, replacing "keyword" with your targeted keyword or industry, and you can find relevant directories for your niche:

keyword + submit
keyword + add url
keyword + add link
keyword + directory
keyword + resources

Here is a short list of business directories to get you started:

http://www.manta.com/claim
http://www.linkedin.com/company/add/show
http://www.hotfrog.com/AddYourBusiness.aspx
http://www.angieslistbusinesscenter.com
http://www.merchantcircle.com/signup
http://www.citysearch.com
https://biz.yelp.com

Stealing competitors' links.

Stealing competitors' links is an old-school tactic receiving a resurgence in recent times, due to Google's increased focus on links from quality sites, making it more difficult to find easy link opportunities.

If your competitor has done all the heavy lifting, why not take advantage of their hard work. Use the below sites to export your competitors' backlinks. By looking through their links you can often find link opportunities to build links pointing to your site. In most cases, you can be confident you are going after SEO-friendly link sources if the competitor is already ranking well in Google.

Ahrefs Backlink Checker – Free to try, then $79 per month.
http://www.ahrefs.com

Majestic SEO Backlink Checker – Free to try, then $49 per month.
https://majestic.com

Open Site Explorer – Free to try, then $99 per month
https://moz.com/researchtools/ose/

Video link building.

Google loves videos, and it especially loves videos from video powerhouse YouTube. If you want the opportunity to capture visitors from the world's largest video search engine, posting videos will considerably help your SEO.

Post relevant how-to guides, industry news updates and instructional videos for the best response from users. Then link to the relevant pages on your site in the description.

The key to success in video link building is to ensure the video and your description are related. You should aim to have your targeted keyword or relevant keywords on the page somewhere.

And don't worry. Your video doesn't have to be on par with the latest Martin Scorsese masterpiece. It can be a simple 5 or 10-minute video, educating visitors with useful knowledge about your topic. Just focus on making it contribute value for the viewer.

The tools below can help with quickly creating videos and uploading them to the web.

CamStudio
http://camstudio.org/
CamStudio is a free, open source screen recording software allowing you to record high-quality screencasts from your own computer. You can download the video files in high quality after you have finished. This product only works on Windows computers, so Mac users may need to find an alternative like Camtasia or SnagIt.

High-quality sites you can easily visit, upload videos and get backlinks from:

http://www.youtube.com
http://www.veoh.com
http://www.dailymotion.com
http://www.metacafe.com
http://www.youku.com
http://www.archive.org

Link bait.

Link bait is a new and effective strategy for building high-quality and powerful links on a large scale. Link bait is great because you create content once, but you can have thousands of people over the Internet sharing and linking to your content, while you sit back and put your feet up.

But what is link bait exactly? Link bait is any kind of compelling content that naturally acquires links from other sites as a result.

While there is an art to creating link bait successfully, you would be surprised at how easy it is to earn links and social media activity with this strategy.

You need to make your content free and shareable. Your content must be so valuable it would almost be worth paying for.

To create this content, you should use your expertise or even hire researchers to put together juicy industry content that lends itself to being shared.

Wrap up this content into a whitepaper, top 10 list, an easy to understand infographic, or a downloadable resource and make it compelling for visitors to read and share.

Promote this content heavily through your site and social media accounts. Prompt readers to share the post at the bottom of the content. Make sharing the content as easy as possible and you will maximize results.

Next up, find popular link bait in your industry or niche.

Then use a link analysis tool such as Ahrefs or Open Site Explorer to pull a list of sites linking to popular content in your niche. Send out a quick email blast to site owners and bloggers to let them know about your bigger and better resource.

If you really want to take link baiting to the next level, write and publish a compelling press release about your link bait content. With a press release, it can be exposed to thousands of journalists and potentially has a chance of attracting media coverage.

You might be wondering what a successful link baiting campaign looks like. I've listed examples below:

WordPress SEO
https://yoast.com/articles/wordpress-seo/
Joost de Valk is well known in the SEO industry, in some part due to his one page guide to WordPress SEO that is updated every month or so. This guide has earned many links and shares over many years.

101 Motivational Business Quotes
http://www.quicksprout.com/2009/12/07/101-motivational-business-quotes/
Excellent example of a great link bait article that went viral, and could be outsourced for pennies on the dollar.

Types of link bait:
- Infographics
- How-to guides
- Beginner guides
- Breaking news

- Top 10 lists
- Industry reports

Pictochart -Free to start
http://www.piktochart.com
Great service for infographic generation, has an easy drag
and drop interface to put infographics together in minutes.

Prlog
http://www.prlog.org
Prlog offers entry-level free press release syndication
services, with additional coverage for an added fee.

PRNewswire
http://www.prnewswire.com
Many PR firms will simply write a press release and then
release it to PRNewswire and charge a premium for doing
so. Cut out the middleman, write up your press release
yourself, and you can get massive PR for a fraction of the
cost of hiring a PR agent. Packages start at $425 USD and
scale up for increased syndication.

Broken link building/link outreach.

Broken link building is a new, but effective strategy. With
this new strategy, you can reach out to quality sites with
broken links on their pages, and use this as an opportunity
to convince the site administrator to provide an updated
link to your site.

When you find a broken link, let them know the broken link exists and you have an alternative resource on your site that will benefit their readers. With this strategy you should create a linkable resource on your site. This makes it very easy for the webmaster to point the link to your replacement.

Use the formulas below to find potential pages with broken links, replacing "keyword" with the keyword you are targeting:

keyword useful links
keyword useful resources
keyword useful sites
keyword recommended links
keyword recommended resources
keyword recommended sites
keyword suggested links
keyword suggested resources
keyword suggested sites
keyword more links
keyword more resources
keyword more sites
keyword related links
keyword related resources
keyword related sites

If you want to automate this process, the service below will do the heavy lifting, and give you a list of sites with broken links and contact details so you can quickly reach out to the webmaster.

Broken linkbuilding - $67 monthly

http://www.brokenlinkbuilding.com
This tool is comprehensive, but comes at a price. By typing in keywords you are targeting, the broken link building tool will find a solid amount of broken link opportunities. Saves time and finds quality opportunities.

Broken brand mentions.

Broken brand mentions is a fast, simple and reliable form of link building you can use for almost every SEO project. It goes like this: in some cases, when someone mentions your brand they forget to post a link. Track mentions of your brand, and where suitable, reach out and ask for a link back to your site. Use the below tools to track mentions of your brand. If you see a mention of your brand without a link, send a quick email to the author, and they will often be happy to link to your site.

Brand monitoring sites I've found useful:

Social Mention -Free to try
http://www.socialmention.com
Social Mention is a very powerful brand monitoring tool. At the writing of this book, you cannot receive email alerts. Social Mention is completely free and powerful, so it's worth checking out.

Mention - Free to try, pricing starts at £29 per month.
https://en.mention.com
Mention is a powerful brand-monitoring tool that will send an email alert when your brand is mentioned online, so you can respond quickly.

Paid links

Paid links are against Google's terms-of-service, these below link building tactics do work and can fly under the radar. Needless to say, if you're feeling daring, you've been warned and I take no responsibility for what happens as a result of paid link strategies.

Donate to charities & non-profits.

Charities and non-profits sites often have a donors page. Search for "site:.org + donors" or "site:.org + sponsors" in Google for a list of organizations that have these pages, offer a donation, and request a listing on the page.

Better Business Bureau.

Links from the Better Business Bureau are among the best links you can receive. Better Business Bureau links will pass authority and trust. Check your listing to see if you are already linking back to your site, and if you're not already a member, then consider signing up.

ADVANCED LINK BUILDING.

The aforementioned link building techniques are enough for about 90% of readers to push rankings higher than competitors. For link building junkies who've exhausted the above options, here's a handful of strategies listed quickly in rapid-fire fashion. These are intended for advanced SEO users, who are actively blogging or have an established social media presence.

1. Create a Twitter profile.

Adding a link in a Twitter profile is a big opportunity disguised as a small opportunity. Simply by creating a Twitter profile, and listing your website in both the "website" and "bio" fields, you will get a handful of links from high domain authority aggregators that scrape your information from Twitter. Sites that do this include Klout, Twellow, Twitter Counter, and many others. To make these links more powerful, you can make your profile active without a large overhead of time. Use a service such as Hootsuite to auto-post blog posts from RSS feeds relevant to your niche, to make your profile active. Build up a base level of followers to your account with a small budget using a service like Twitter Ads or Twitter Counter - Featured Users.

Hootsuite
http://www.hootsuite.com

Twitter Ads
https://ads.twitter.com

Twitter Counter – Featured Users
http://twittercounter.com/pages/featured

2. Pingback & trackback link building targeting authority sites.

You can get a handful of easy-win authority links, including .edu and .gov links, by linking out to blogs in your industry with pingbacks enabled. Pingbacks are notifications from your blog sent to other blogs when you mention an external post. Blogs with pingbacks enabled will show a link back to your website in their comment section when this happens.

Here's how a comment will look if it is a trackback or pingback:

Digital nomad blog
[…]read the latest tips on how to travel with only your carry on luggage[…]

Pingbacks build up valuable relevant links back to your website. They can also be a traffic source, picking up engaged readers from other sites and sending them to your site.

Run a quick search on Google to find the top-50 or top-100 blogs in your industry, then go through and find the ones with trackbacks enabled. For example, to find digital nomad blogs, you might type into Google:

intitle:"digital nomad" "comment"

Next up, in your upcoming blog posts, link out to blogs with pingbacks enabled. For this to work successfully, keep in mind you need to link out to actual posts, not the home page.

3. Create your own authority links.

The most powerful link building strategy is to simply go out and make your own authority links. By buying a previously owned website or domain, you can turn it into a blog and unlimited source for powerful, highly relevant links back to your site.

There are readers out there who will scoff at this strategy and there are readers out there nodding their heads — it's the readers nodding their heads that know how powerful this strategy is. Links from authority sources in your market are much more powerful than any other kind of link, and the easiest way to get authority links is to create your own authority site. Consider buying a website more than three or four years old with a relevant domain, for a more powerful effect.

Be careful with this strategy. If you create a network of sites like this and obscure the ownership details at the domain registry, and only link back to websites you own, you risk being labeled as the owner of a private-blog-network by Google and could potentially receive ranking penalties. However, if you create a legitimate, authoritative resource that creates genuine value for users you should be fine.

Flippa
https://flippa.com
Market place for buying and selling websites.

Sedo
https://sedo.com
Buy and sell domains.

4. Relationship link building.

If you've been following the online advice on blogging and link building in the past couple of years you will have noticed a recurring theme: building relationships with other bloggers in your industry is a powerful way to earn strong backlinks to your site.

While this strategy is only relevant for users with active blogs on their site, fortunately, creating these relationships and getting the links is easier than it sounds. Other bloggers in your industry are just as dependent on links as you are. By linking out in your blog posts to other bloggers you 1) give a valuable backlink to the blogger, and 2) give recognition to the blogger for being an authority in the industry. Everyone likes recognition, and the law of reciprocity comes into play here, you will find most bloggers are grateful for being mentioned and happy to link back in a social media post or future blog post.

Try creating or curating popular blog posts into a top-level summary, then send a quick email to the bloggers mentioned, let them know, and very politely ask for a mention or linkback. The best part of this strategy is curating blog posts; it is often easier than creating content from scratch.

Example email:
Hey [expert blogger],
Just thought I'd give you a heads up. I've just featured you in my post [xyz]...

Hope you don't mind. If you're happy with the article, I would really appreciate a mention on social media or perhaps a link back. Or if you want anything changed, feel free to let me know.

Really enjoyed your post on [xyz].

Thanks!

Example expert round-up post:
Experienced business travellers reveal their favorite travel tips
http://www.businessinsider.sg/business-travel-tips-from-expert-travelers-2015-6/

5. Testimonial link building.

An awesome way to get high quality, relevant links back to your site is to give out testimonials. Sometimes you can actually earn a link back to your site from somebody else's homepage, possibly one of the strongest types of links to get! I will sometimes go far as purchasing a product just to get a testimonial link. Give this strategy a try by finding a few sites with testimonials and offering your own. Of course make it easy for the webmaster by including all the information they need, such as a photo, your name, job title, testimonial and link back to your site. The key is to look for businesses or services with a testimonials page already, or a testimonials carousel or widget on their homepage. Speed up your search with a couple of Google search queries:

"keyword" +testimonials
"keyword" +recommendations
"keyword" +"client testimonials"

"keyword" +"what customers say"
"keyword" +"what our customers say"

SOCIAL MEDIA & SEO.

IS SOCIAL MEDIA IMPORTANT FOR SEO?

Social media has become integral to the way we use the Internet. Important content is not only linked, it is shared, liked, tweeted and pinned. How people use the Internet has drastically changed, and this hasn't gone unnoticed at the Googleplex. Many of the independent studies on Google's ranking algorithm show a large correlation with high-ranking pages having strong social media activity.

While the official stance from Google is that they do not directly use social signals in their algorithm, the SEO community pretty much agrees it is certainly a factor in achieving rankings. Disagreements aside, I can tell from my own experience, sites with large social followings consistently get higher rankings in a shorter timeframe.

Not only can you use social media to build social activity to increase your overall SEO strength, you can use social media to regularly create backlinks that are free and easy to build. It also increases referral traffic back to your site and engages previous customers. As a rule, social media should be a part of every SEO project, or even every marketing project.

GOOGLE+ & SEO.

Google has been consistently rewarding businesses using their own social network with higher rankings. To be specific, Google+ is reported as one of strongest ranking factors for the past several years, so much so, if you look at the SEO ranking factor surveys, Google+ is consistently at the top of the list!

A lot of businesses still aren't using Google+, so this is an opportunity to get an advantage over competitors. At a minimum, you should set up a business page and add some posts to your profile. Next up, encourage followers by adding a Google+ follow button on your website, and link to your Google+ page in your email footer. Social media management is beyond the scope of this book, but simply getting started and building a base level of activity on Google+ will put yourself ahead of other businesses — it is the social media site most often overlooked by many brands, and you can use this to your advantage. Get started with the below links:

Google+
https://plus.google.com

Google+ Follow Button
https://developers.google.com/+/web/follow/

FACEBOOK & SEO.

Facebook is the world's most popular social network. What's popular on Facebook is essentially a snapshot of public opinion, and Google have noted this by making Facebook activity a very strong factor in their algorithm. You should consider using Facebook for every SEO project. If you only have the time or budget to use one social network in your SEO strategy, use Facebook.

To improve your site's Facebook social activity, share content from your own site on your Facebook page on a regular basis.

Each time you do this, you receive more exposure from your fan base, and you also build up social activity around the content on your site. Be careful to mix this up with relevant, engaging non-commercial content for your user base, so you don't turn them off and maintain high levels of engagement. Examples include infographics, inspirational quotes, inspirational photos, and so on.

Build up your audience by including a Facebook follow button on your site, your email signatures, and your thank you or success pages.

If you want to speed up building your audience, you can use Facebook advertising to build a relevant audience of local customers. This is a good strategy if your competitors in the rankings have a larger following and you are looking to beat them. You can also use Facebook advertising to increase exposure for your posts, or even run advertising campaigns for a promotional offer. Facebook advertising stands out as a great way to build up an audience, social activity and referral sales for projects with a budget.

Facebook for business
https://www.facebook.com/business

Facebook advertising
https://en-gb.facebook.com/business/products/ads

TWITTER & SEO.

Twitter is filled with discussion on the world's latest news and events. In many cases, groundbreaking news stories are released on Twitter before the world's major news outlets. The death of Osama Bin Laden is the perfect example — it was leaked on Twitter by a former chief of staff to the US Defense Secretary and within minutes it was all over the news.

Google have recognized this and use Twitter activity in their algorithm. While it may not be as strong as other social networks, you can use Twitter to build up your overall SEO strength. Twitter is a great social network to weave into your SEO strategy as you can schedule a lot of your tweets in advance without coming across as too spammy, and manage your account with only a small commitment of time and effort.

Schedule tweets to your pages such as Hootsuite and start building up your tweet counts on your pages. Mix this up with relevant and informative tweets about your industry. You should aim for a maximum of 12 tweets per day. 12 Tweets per day is roughly the limit you can post without annoying your followers. If you're lazy like me, you can schedule all of your tweets about 3-months in advance.

If you want to encourage site visitors to tweet your content for you, include a "tweet this page" link on every page or blog post on your web site.

Tweetdeck -Free
http://www.tweetdeck.com

Free and easy Twitter management software. You can install Tweetdeck on your computer and manage your whole Twitter account from inside the program. Popular features include managing multiple accounts, scheduling tweets, and arranging feeds so you only see updates from Twitterers you're interested in.

Hootsuite -Free to start. $10 monthly for power users.
http://www.hootsuite.com

More advanced than Tweetdeck, you can use Hootsuite to schedule tweets, analyze social media traffic, manage multiple accounts, create social media reports to monitor your success, and much more. Recommended for power users or automating multiple accounts.

OTHER SOCIAL NETWORKS.

Let's face it, we'd all love to play around on social networks all day, but we don't have the spare time to be always looking for great ideas and sharing them endlessly on social media accounts.

If you have limited resources, focus on Facebook, Google+ and Twitter.

If you are looking for an extra edge, doing SEO for a large brand, or maybe you have an army of helpers waiting for your command, you can gain significant boosts by expanding your social activity to several social media sites.

Setup an account on the below networks, posting on the networks most relevant to your business:

LinkedIn
http://www.linkedin.com

LinkedIn is the Facebook for professionals. LinkedIn is a fantastic networking tool if you are in the business-to-business industry and looking to build up your personal brand or the brand of your site. If you want to increase your effectiveness on Linkedin, join groups and participate in discussions, post relevant updates about your industry and post content in the news feed.

Pinterest
http://www.pinterest.com

Pinterest has become one of the fastest-growing social networks in a very short timeframe. Pinterest's fast-growing user base is primarily made up of women. The site has effectively turned into a giant shopping list of wish-list items. If your target audience is women, you should be on Pinterest.

Instagram
http://www.instagram.com

Initially a mobile app to help users make their photos look pretty, Instagram has skyrocketed from a fledgling mobile app to competing with major social networks in just a few years. Instagram limits the amount of links you can post, which essentially means the links from your profile on Instagram are much more powerful. If you work in a fashion or image-heavy industry, Instagram is a must-have social network to incorporate into your SEO and overall digital strategy.

SOCIAL MEDIA ANALYTICS.

If you invest time and effort building up your social media profiles, you will want to track your results so you can separate the parts of your strategy that are successful and not so successful.

Social media analytics is different compared to other web analytics, because social analytics are geared to measuring the conversation and interaction of your fan base with your brand. Using the software listed below, you can monitor results and get valuable insights on how to improve your social media efforts:

Sprout Social - Free for 30-days. $59 per month for regular use.
http://sproutsocial.com/features
Sprout Social is a great web analytics and social media management package that allows you to track the performance of your social media profiles over time. It has a free trial, suited to advanced level use and offers powerful analytic reports for major social networks.

Hootsuite - Free plan available. Paid plans start at $10 per month.
https://hootsuite.com/products/social-media-analytics

Hootsuite is quoted many times in this book and for good reason—Hootsuite is a robust social media management software allowing for control over many social networks, as well as powerful web analytics insights. Its paid plans are also quite affordable for pro-users.

Google Analytics Social Tracking - Free
http://www.google.com/analytics/

Google Analytics social-tracking features are great for tracking basic social interactions that occur when visitors are on your site. It is free and includes an out-of-the-box solution with the standard setup. To see social reports, log in to Google Analytics, click on the "Acquisition" tab in the main menu, then "Social".

WEB ANALYTICS IN A NUTSHELL. HOW TO MEASURE YOUR SUCCESS.

Web analytics changed how we do business in the 21st century. Now we can find valuable insights into customers, including what was previously difficult or impossible to discover, including information on website visitors' demographics, interests, online behaviors, and more. We can find out what works and what doesn't, cut under performing marketing campaigns and increase budgets for winning campaigns. Simply put, web analytics have made it easier to grow almost any business. Read on for a quick guide covering the nuts and bolts of web analytics, and how to put web analytics to work for your business.

WHY USE GOOGLE ANALYTICS?

You may have already heard about Google Analytics. Google Analytics is the web analytics platform used by the majority of sites. It has its quirks, but it's the best readily available, all-round analytics tool available for understanding site traffic. And the best part is it's free.

If you don't have Google Analytics installed, put down this book, install Google Analytics now and then slap your web developer. I'm not joking. Without Google Analytics set up, growing a business online is like trying to pilot an airplane blindfolded. Without Google Analytics it's difficult to find out what works and what doesn't, identify issues and solve them before they turn into bigger issues, and get a sense for the general direction your business is headed. Google Analytics is usefulness for monitoring the performance of a business and is applicable to about 95% of businesses.

To get started with Google Analytics, head on over to the below URL and click on "sign in". Create a Google account if you do not have one already, and walk through the simple steps to get started. You may need help from your web developer if you are unable to edit the code on your website.

Google Analytics
http://www.google.com/analytics/

HOW TO USE GOOGLE ANALYTICS.

Let me tell you something a little risqué. On its own, most data is useless. You heard correctly, for real awareness and insights, we need to be able to compare data and identify trends over time. There are two ways to analyze and understand data in Google Analytics in reference to time:

1. Compare two date ranges.

Click on the date field input in Google Analytics. Enter two timeframes and you can compare them both. Useful date comparisons include comparing this week's performance to last week's performance, last month's performance to the month prior, and last month's performance to the same month the previous year.

2. Look at the charts over a long time frame.

Simply look at the charts over the longest time period possible and look for trends, without comparing date ranges. This is not so effective for finding hard-to-find information or identifying granular insights, but this approach is useful for a bird's eye view of the direction your traffic is heading.

Note: Seasonality is a factor affecting many businesses. Sometimes you may see a downturn in traffic, but this may not necessarily indicate your site is performing poorly. It could be that your market experiences a downward trend in certain months. If your business is experiencing a downward trend, use the "compare two date ranges" approach and compare the current month's traffic to the same month last year. If you are seeing increases, then you know your site is performing well, irrespective of seasonal trends.

ACQUISITION.

Acquisition is an area of Google Analytics any business owner or marketer should spend a lot of time reviewing. The Acquisition section of Google Analytics breaks down where your site traffic is coming from. Without keeping a close eye on your traffic sources, it is almost impossible to make informed judgments about the performance of your site or your marketing.

Click "Acquisition" in the main sidebar on the left. In the "All Traffic" section you can see actual amounts of traffic you've received from a given source. The Channels section listed under "All Traffic" is of special interest. This lists the main sources sending customers to your website. From the "Channels" tab, you can dig further for deeper insights into the performance for specific sources sending customers to your site, such as social visitors, search engine visitors, email visitors, and so on.

ORGANIC SEARCH REPORT

The Organic Search report is essential for monitoring your performance in search engines. Within the Organic Search report, you can actually see how many times you received a visitor from a search engine.

It's worth mentioning, a few years ago Google made changes to Google Analytics that still has many search engine marketers and marketing professionals shaking their fists at the sky. Early in 2012, Google changed this tool to hide a large portion of the keyword information, making it difficult to get exact information on the keywords customers are using to arrive at your site. Thanks Google!

Now when someone types a phrase into Google, if they are signed into a Google account while browsing, the keyword the visitor searches for will show up as a "not provided" keyword in Google Analytics report. When this happens, you have no idea what that person typed into Google before arriving at your site.

The amount of keyword information that has been obscured by Google has gradually increased, but don't be too concerned, we can still measure overall performance of search engine traffic by looking for total increases or decreases in the Organic Search report.

To view the Organic Search report, click on the Acquisition tab on the left sidebar, click on "All Traffic", click on "Channels", and click on "Organic Search".

SEGMENTS.

Imagine if you could narrow down to a particular segment of your audience, such as paid traffic, search engine traffic, mobile traffic, iPad users, and so on, and instantly see how many inquiries these users have made, how much time they are spending on your site, what country they are from, and how many sales they are making. This feature exists and it is called Segments.

Segments are powerful. With Segments, you can identify portions of your audience that potentially generate more inquiries or sales than other customers. You can even identify portions of your audience having difficulty using your site, and get insights to fix these areas for better performance.

To use Segments, simply click on the "Add Segment" tab at the top of every page within Google Analytics, and you can choose from the list a large number of Segments for deeper insights.

COMMON WEB ANALYTICS TERMS EXPLAINED.

Pageviews.

A Pageview is counted each time a user loads a page on your site.

Unique Pageviews.

Similar to a Pageview, but if one user loads a page several times it will only be considered one Unique Pageview.

Session.

A session is what occurs when a visitor arrives at the site, and then at some point closes the browser. If that visitor returns again, this is counted as an additional session.

User.

If a user visits your site, and then returns at a later stage, this is counted as one unique User.

Bounce Rate.

If a visitor visits your site, and then leaves without visiting any more pages, this is a bounce. The percentage of visitors who bounce is your bounce rate. A common question among marketers and business owners is: what is a good bounce rate? There is no general rule. Bounce rates vary greatly between sites and industries. If you find a particular page with a very high bounce rate (+70%), this could be an indicator the visitors do not like the content or they are experiencing technical issues.

Conversion rate.

One of the most important metrics to monitor is your site conversion rate. A conversion rate is the percentage of Users completing a desired action. The action could be filling out an inquiry form, downloading a product, or buying something from you. If you receive one hundred visitors, and three of these visitors complete a sale, this would be a three percent conversion rate.

Goals.

Goals are custom goals you can set up within Google Analytics to track particular business goals or targets you may have for your site.

Common goals to set up include newsletter signups, product downloads, inquiry form completions, and so on.

OTHER WEB ANALYTICS TOOLS.

There are many web analytics tools out there to help with improving the performance of your site. Google Analytics is great for understanding overall traffic performance, but if you want to delve deeper, check out the following tools for greater insights:

Crazy Egg - Free to start. Starts at $108 per year for premium features. Requires a Google Account to get started.
http://www.crazyegg.com

If you want a visual indication of how visitors behave on your site once they arrive, Crazy Egg is a fantastic tool. With Crazy Egg, you can get heat maps of where visitors click on the page. You can also see heat maps of how far visitors scroll down the page.

Optimizely - Free for basic users.
http://www.optimizely.com

Optimizely is a popular split-testing analytics tool. With Optimizely you can split test different variations of your site, and see which version makes more sales or conversions.

TROUBLESHOOTING COMMON SEO PROBLEMS & HOW TO FIX THEM.

Dealing with Google can be massively frustrating at times. Customer support barely exists, and trying to understand why your site isn't playing well with Google can spiral into a wild goose chase.

Don't let Google's lack of customer support or the horror stories dishearten you. Most of the time, if a site is experiencing Google problems, it is only temporary. SEO problems are rarely irrecoverable.

Usually it's simply a matter of finding out the underlying cause of the problem—more often than not, the cause isn't what the popular blog posts are saying it might be. This sometimes means fixing several items. Once all fixed, you have stacked the deck in your favor and you are more likely to make a speedy recovery.

This chapter outlines common SEO problems that plague web site owners.

If you are not at all technically inclined, I urge you to read the section on getting additional advice, or even consider getting professional help if your site is experiencing serious SEO issues.

WHAT TO DO WHEN YOUR SITE IS NOT LISTED IN GOOGLE AT ALL.

This is a common problem among webmasters and business owners alike.

If you have just launched a brand new site, it is possible Google has not crawled your site yet. You can do a quick spot check by typing "site:yoursiteaddress.com" into the Google search bar and checking to see if your site comes up at all. If it doesn't, it's possible Google's spider hasn't crawled your site and doesn't know it exists.

Typically all that's required for Google to pick up your site is to generate a handful of links to your site, and some social activity.

Tweeting a link to your site is a quick way to ensure your site is indexed by Google's software, typically within 24 hours. Try to share your site from a handful of social networks for faster results.

Check Google again in 24 hours with the "site:www.yoursite…" search query and see if any pages from your site come up. If you do see pages, this means Google has indexed your site.

If this doesn't work, ask your web designer to setup Google Search Console for you, login and see if there are any errors. If there are errors, Google will outline the steps to fix them, so Google can see your site.

WHAT TO DO WHEN YOUR BUSINESS IS NOT RANKING FOR YOUR OWN BUSINESS NAME.

A business not coming up in the top position in Google for searches for the official business name is a surprisingly common issue among brand new sites. Google is smart, but sometimes you need to give Google a nudge to associate your new site with the name of your brand.

This solution is easily fixed by building links to your site, with some of the links with your brand name as the anchor text. This can take up to a couple of weeks for Google to see these links, connect the dots and realize your site is the real deal.

The fast way to get the ball rolling is to do a quick search for the business directories used in your country — Whitepages, Yellow Pages, Yelp, and so on — fill out a listing for your business on each site and include a link back to your web site. The more links the better, but you should be aiming for a minimum of 50 links. In 95% of cases, this will solve the problem of a site not coming up in the top results of searches for the business name.

If this doesn't work, setup Facebook and Twitter accounts for your business, filling out as much information about your business as possible in the profile. Then do a post a day for about two weeks, mixing in links to your site in the posts.

If you still can't get your site ranking high enough, use Open Site Explorer to spy on competing sites ranking higher for the brand name. Do their pages have more backlinks than the total amount of links to your site? If this is the case, you are going to need to build more links.

WHAT TO DO WHEN YOUR RANKINGS HAVE DROPPED OFF.

Here's a sad truth about SEO: if you achieve a top ranking, it may not keep its position forever. There are billions of web pages competing for top positions in Google. New sites are being created every day. It requires an ongoing effort to keep pages ranking high.

If your rankings have dropped off from the top position, and are slowly moving their way down the search results, it's likely your competitors have simply acquired more links or more social activity. Use Open Site Explorer to spy on competitors, find out how many backlinks they have, how much social media activity they have, and set these amounts as your target to build your rankings back up.

Next, it's time to start a link building campaign with the targeted keywords as outlined in the chapter on link building.

If you are worried that you may have been penalized by the recent updates to Google, such as the Penguin update or the Panda update, read the next section for common recovery steps.

WHAT TO DO WHEN YOUR SITE HAS BEEN PENALIZED BY A PENGUIN UPDATE.

The recent updates to Google have many site owners worried. The media circus are partly to blame for this, but the controversy surrounding the Panda and Penguin updates created the misconception that most traffic issues are caused by these updates.

The real truth — these updates have affected a fraction of sites and these site owners are a very loud minority.

In most cases, if your rankings have dropped off, your competitors have simply acquired more "SEO Juice" to their pages, and it's time to pick up your game. If your pages have moved down a few positions, refer to the above section on the steps to recovery.

If your rankings have completely disappeared from Google's top 30, and they were previously ranking in the top 10, then it is possible you may have been penalized from Google's Penguin update. Follow the below steps to confirm if this was the case and follow the recommended steps to make a recovery.

Read on with caution. Penalties from the Panda and Penguin updates are difficult to diagnose and even more difficult to heal. If you are out of your depth, you may need to seek professional help to make a speedy recovery.

1. Check Google Search Console.

Any site owners that have had a *manual* penalty imposed on Google will receive a notice like the one below. Log in to your Google Search Console account to see if you have received a notice like one of the examples below:

'Google Search Console notice of detected unnatural links to....'

We've detected that some of your site's pages may be using techniques that are outside of Google's Webmaster Guidelines....'

If you have witnessed the above message in Google Search Console, Google has placed a manual penalty on your site as a result of the new Google updates. If you do not see the above message, then it is unlikely you have received a manual penalty from Google.

2. Check your link profile.

Use Open Site Explorer, and Majestic SEO and look at the links pointing to the page you suspect may have been penalized. Do the same for the competing pages that are currently ranking in the top position for your keywords.

Look for the indicators below to confirm if your site has been penalized by the Google updates.

1. Your site has a much larger quantity of links than competitors, but isn't ranking in the top 50 for the same keyword.

If you have a significantly larger amount of links pointing to your page than competing sites, and your site is nowhere to be seen in the top 50 (but it was before), then you may have been penalized by the Penguin update.

2. Your site has a very large quantity of links from shoddy looking sites, e.g. sites that look like the following, seolinksdirectory.com, addurlsfree.com, freelinkdirectory.com, and so on.

3. Your page has anchor text pointing to the page for your targeted keyword greater than 20% as a general rule. Example: if 90% of the links pointing to the page have a targeted keyword as the anchor text, it is possible you may have been penalized by the Penguin update.

4. Use the Panguin tool to see if you have any sudden traffic declines around the times of the Google updates. If your traffic has not recovered, then it is possible your site has been penalized by Penguin.

Panguin tool
http://barracuda.digital/panguin-tool/

Google Penguin recovery steps

The following list walks you through the process required to heal a site penalized by Google Penguin. Please note, before you do any of these items, you must be absolutely confident your site has been affected by these updates. If your site has not been penalized by these updates, the below steps could do more harm than good to your site. If you are certain, it is highly recommended you seek professional advice.

1. Export all the backlinks to the page that has been penalized, using your Google Search Console account, Open Site Explorer and Majestic SEO. Compile all of the links together into an Excel spreadsheet.

Go through and group together the links on spammy domains (e.g. freelinks.tv, seolinksdirectory.com, freeseolinks.com, bizlinks.biz and so on).

2. Visit each of these spammy sites and look for a link removal page. If there is no link removal page, find a contact page and request the site administrator to remove your link from their site. Provide a link to the page in your message to make it easier for the webmaster.

If you cannot locate any contact information for the site, use Domain Whois to find the site owner's contact details and contact the owner directly.

Domain Whois
http://whois.domaintools.com/

Document all of these efforts in a spreadsheet with a date, time and outcome.

3. After you have allowed one to two weeks for the webmasters to remove the links to your site, find the spammy links for the sites you have not been able to remove and put each of these bad links into a plain text file, with each link placed on a new line.

Log into Google Search Console and submit these links using the "Remove URLs" page in the "Optimization" section. Again, if you are uncertain about what you are doing, consult a professional SEO otherwise you could risk doing more harm than good.

4. File a reconsideration request in Google Search Console. This should only occur after you have made a very thorough effort to remove your links manually and then disavowed the links through the disavow link tool.

You must submit a request to Google to let them know you believe you have been blocked by the Penguin update, and have gone to great efforts to clean up the link spam.

To do this, visit the following URL after logging into your Google Search Console account:

File a reconsideration request
https://www.google.com/webmasters/tools/reconsideration?pli=1

5. Await response and monitor rankings changes.

As mentioned, recovering from a Google Penguin penalty is not something anybody should do without a base level of professional SEO experience and complete confidence the site has been penalized by the Penguin update.

These steps have been included for those with SEO experience, and to illustrate the steps required to recover from a Penguin penalty.

It is highly recommended you speak with an expert before doing any of the above to attempt to recover from a penalty.

HOW TO SEEK PROFESSIONAL HELP FOR FREE.

Finding the right SEO help can be frustrating for site owners. There is a lot of information to navigate, with varying levels of quality and accuracy. It's difficult to get in touch with SEO practitioners at the top of their field.

That said, there are sites that can put your questions in front of world-leading experts of almost any topic for free. Use the below sites for highly technical responses, and you can create an army of Internet experts to try to solve your problem for you.

The key to success with the below resources is to be specific. The more specific you are, and the more information you provide, you increase your chances you will receive a detailed answer that will point you in the right direction.

For greater results, post your question on *all* of the sites below, and sit back and wait for the answers to come in. You will get more answers and will be in a better position to consider which solution is best.

Moz Q&A
http://moz.com/community/q

Moz's Q&A forums used to be private, but eventually recently released this feature open to the public. Here you can speak with a large number of SEO professionals directly and attract high quality answers to your questions. Great for SEO specific problems.

Pro Webmasters
http://webmasters.stackexchange.com

The Pro Webmasters Q&A board can have your questions answered by webmasters of high-performing sites.

Quora
http://www.quora.com

Quora is an all-round Q&A posting board, where you can get a question answered on almost anything. On Quora, questions are often answered by high-profile experts. Marketers, business owners, you name it, there are many leading industry authorities posting answers to questions on Quora.

Stack Overflow
http://stackoverflow.com

Created by the founders of Pro Webmasters, Stack Overflow is a community of web developers answering web development related questions. If you have a very technical question related to your site, or if you just want to keep your web developer honest by getting a second opinion, Stack Overflow is a great resource for getting highly technical questions answered.

Wordpress Answers
http://wordpress.stackexchange.com

If your site is built on Wordpress, it's inevitable you will eventually encounter some kind of technical hurdle. The Wordpress Answers Q&A board is a great resource to seek out help.

Indexing & SERP Display Problems and Questions
High Rankings Forum
http://www.highrankings.com/forum/index.php/forum/67-indexing-and-serp-display-problems-and-questions/

This discussion board on the High Rankings forum is specifically related to users having trouble getting their site to rank in Google. Here you will find answers for tough questions with a fast turnaround time. As is the case with all discussion boards, you can have a lively discussion about any topic, but you should always cross-reference and verify any information you receive.

LOCAL SEO. SEO FOR LOCAL BUSINESSES.

WHY USE LOCAL SEO?

Unless you have been living under a rock, you have seen listings for local business appearing at the top of some search results in Google. Local listings — previously known as Google Place page listings, now known as Google+ pages — are a powerful marketing tool for small businesses.

Let's look at some statistics from the horse's mouth. The below facts were discovered by Google after conducting a study on the behavior of local customers.
- 4 in 5 consumers use search engines to find local information.*
- 50% of consumers who conducted a local search on their smartphone visited a store within a day.*
- 18% of local searches on a smartphone lead to a purchase within a day.*

* Understanding Consumer's Local Search Behavior – May, 2014
https://think.storage.googleapis.com/docs/how-advertisers-can-extend-their-relevance-with-search_research-studies.pdf

Holy mackerel, if you are a local business owner and those figures aren't making your jaw drop, I don't know what will. Now that we know if you own a local business local search can be the Yoko Ono to your John Lennon, let's delve a little deeper and find out what makes up a local search result.

Local search results differ from traditional organic search results by representing a local business instead of a normal web page, and appearing at the top of the search results and on map listings.

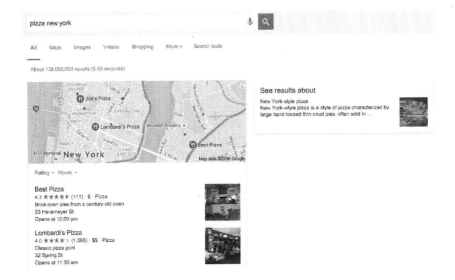

Users can get business contact details, opening hours and reviews and find the information they need quickly and easily, instead of having to dig around a clunky business site.

The local listings can be a powerful tool to attract traffic. In many cases, local listings can lead to many more inquiries than regular SEO rankings. But does this mean you should scrap traditional SEO in favor of local SEO? Nope. You can do both and potentially double the amount of potential traffic you can receive.

HOW TO RANK HIGH WITH LOCAL SEO.

Ranking high with local SEO takes a different approach than traditional SEO. Google's algorithm is looking for a different set of signals to determine the popularity of a business to decide how high to rank it in the search results.

If you think about it, if a restaurant is really popular in a city, a whole bunch of links from all over the world probably isn't the best factor to determine how valuable the business is to the local area.

A better indicator of the importance would be mentions of the business's name and phone number across the web, customer reviews, and details on the website that show the business is based in the area being searched.

Below is a list of the most important ranking factors Google use for local listings:

1. Proximity of address to the area being searched.
2. Physical address in city of search.
3. Proper Google My Business category associations.
4. Quality and authority of inbound links.

5. Consistency of citations on primary sources (Google My Business, your website, etc)
6. Domain authority of website.
7. Quality and authority of structured citations.
8. Product/service keyword in Google My Business title.
9. Consistency of citations on secondary citation sources (external business directories, etc)
10. Click-through rate from search results.

These are the strongest factors fetched from Moz's annual Local Search Ranking Factors survey. If you want to rank high in the local search results, all you have to do is ensure your site and Google My Business page have more of these features than your competitors.

For a complete breakdown of local SEO ranking factors, visit the below link, where the world's leading authorities on local SEO publish an industry survey on the local ranking factors every year.

Moz's Local Search Ranking Factors
https://moz.com/local-search-ranking-factors

GETTING STARTED WITH LOCAL SEO.

To get started, the first step is to create your business page on Google My Business. Visit the URL below, and complete every area of your profile as possible. This means creating a detailed description of your business, available payment methods, and so on. The more information you complete, the more you increase your chances of ranking your page higher.

Google My Business
https://www.google.com/business

When creating your business listing, make sure you choose the most accurate category for your business, e.g. if you provide plumbing as a service, you want to choose "plumbing" as your category, not "trades" or "home repairs".

BUILDING CITATIONS.

Citations are the links of local SEO. A citation occurs each time your name, address, phone number (NAP) is mentioned on the web. The more citations you have, the more likely your site will rank high. The easiest places to build citations are the many local business directories available for businesses.

While there's many online directories for creating business listings, the following websites would be a good start for a US-based business.

https://www.facebook.com/business
https://www.linkedin.com/
https://www.yellowpages.com/
https://biz.yelp.com/
http://www.local.com/
http://www.whitepages.com/business
http://www.manta.com/
http://www.citysearch.com
https://foursquare.com/business/
http://www.merchantcircle.com/

BUILDING REVIEWS.

Citations and reviews are the link building of local SEO. If you are only building citations, you only have half of the equation covered. To rank highly, you need to ensure your business accumulates online reviews.

Many businesses struggle with this. This is because it's tough to get customers to fill out reviews! You have to make it easy for your customers.

Include links to your business Google My Business page on your site, email signatures, flyers, and business cards, prompting customers to leave a review. Encourage customers at the end of each sale or transaction to leave a review. By creating every opportunity possible for customers to leave a review, you can significantly increase reviews.

But whatever you do, don't buy reviews. This is a quick way to get into Google's naughty books. Purchased reviews can be picked up by Google's filters and are likely to be excluded from your business profile anyways.

LOCAL SEO RANKING CHECKLIST & ESSENTIAL RESOURCES.

While looking at your local competitors and working to beat them is probably the best overall strategy, progressing through the following checklist will put you on your way to ranking high at the top of the local search results.

1. Verify your business profile on Google My Business.
2. Fill out as much information as possible on your Google My Business profile, including description, category associations, images and videos.
3. Include your business name and location somewhere on your website, this could be your contact page or home page.
4. Include your full business name, address and phone somewhere on your site, these should be grouped together so Google will register it as a citation.
5. Include the appropriate schema.org tags in your website markup, following their specification for local businesses at the following URL.
    Schema.org Local Business Specifications.
    https://schema.org/LocalBusiness
6. Encourage customers to review your business.
7. Submit your website to the major business directories like Yelp, Yellow Pages, CitySearch and so on. You can use tools like Moz Local to submit your business to all of the major directories in one go.
    Moz Local.

https://moz.com/local

8. Cross-check your business listings for correct NAP data. These details need to be consistent across your Google My Business listing, website contact page, and external business listings.

A downloadable copy of the above steps is also available in the SEO checklist at the end of the book.

Essential local SEO resources for keeping up to date.

Just like traditional SEO, local SEO constantly changes and becomes more complex over time. To keep your skills sharp you need to stay up to date with the latest knowledge in the industry. The resources below should be considered essential reading for anyone looking to hone their local SEO skill set.

Local SEO Guide
http://www.localseoguide.com/

Andrew Shotland's Local SEO Guide is an enduring commentary of local SEO techniques and updates in the industry. His useful blog has been around for as long as local SEO has been a thing and is popular among the SEO community for good reason — the author's regular contributions and willingness to give away valuable and actionable advice.

Understanding Google My Business & Local Search
http://blumenthals.com/blog/

Mike Blumenthal is another stalwart blogger providing a running commentary on local SEO. This is a great resource for keeping abreast of the very latest changes in the local search space as they are rolled out.

Moz Local Learning Center
https://moz.com/learn/local

The pre-eminent pundits at Moz have compiled a very useful and detailed guide for managing all aspects of local marketing. Their guide is both extensive and easy to read, making it a great resource for both beginners and advanced practitioners.

THE NEW META: MICROFORMATS, MICRODATA, SCHEMA.ORG & FACEBOOK OPEN GRAPH.

MICROFORMATS, RDFA, MICRODATA & SCHEMA.ORG. WHERE TO START?

A growing problem has emerged on the Internet in the past couple of years. There's literally billions of sites and webpages with an infinite amount of information — all completely unorganized... A bureaucratic nightmare!

There are endless pages about movies, customer reviews, local businesses, product catalogs, and so on, and there has been no standardized way of organizing or presenting this information.

A need emerged for a universal method to make it easy for search engines to quickly recognize this information.

Hence the birth of meta data or semantic data markup — new technologies that can be used on your site making it easier for search engines — and other technologies — to crawl, recognize and present your content to Internet users.

Considering banging your head against the wall, wondering why you're reading such a soul-destroyingly dry topic? Well, don't throw this book out the window just yet...

These new technologies mean you can have greater control over your search listings, make it easier for search engines to crawl your site, and achieve "rich snippets' like the example below, with which you can achieve higher click-through rates and get more eyeballs on your content. Think of this new technology like meta description tags on steroids.

Slipknot Tickets | **Slipknot Concert** Tickets & Tour Dates ...
www.ticketmaster.com › ... › Hard Rock/Metal ▾ Ticketmaster ▾
Results 1 - 10 of 21 - Buy Slipknot tickets from the official Ticketmaster.com site. Find
Slipknot tour schedule, concert details, reviews and photos.

Sat, Oct 25	KNOTFEST - SATURDAY ...	San Manuel Amphitheater ...
Sat, Oct 25	Knotfest - 2 Day Pass	San Manuel Amphitheater ...
Sun, Oct 26	KNOTFEST - SUNDAY Single ...	San Manuel Amphitheater ...

WHY USE SCHEMA.ORG

So now we know what we can do with this new technology, where do we start? As always with new technologies, there's an ongoing debate about the best to use — RDFa, microdata, hCards, microformats, the list goes on.

Well I won't waste your time with a technical debate. Google, Yahoo and Bing joined together in 2011 to hit the data nail on the head and created a standardized approach with schema.org — a reference site for the Microdata markup technology, which allows you to cover all of your meta-data needs.

Google openly stated Microdata, and it's sister-site schema.org, is their preferred technology, and made it clear not to mix meta data technologies for fear of confusing their spider.

We're here for high rankings and traffic, not a lengthy diatribe on each individual technology, so let's go with what Google recommends for the purposes of this book.

HOW TO USE SCHEMA.ORG.

Google supports the below custom listings in the search results. If you have any of the below, your site can benefit from use of schema.org's recommended additional markup for your site.

- Reviews
- People
- Products
- Businesses and organizations

- Recipes
- Events
- Music
- Video content

We'll use an example of a business listing to see how it might normally be coded, compared to following schema.org's recommendation.

Standard code for business details

```
<h1>Beachwalk Beachwear & Giftware</h1>
<p>A superb collection of fine gifts and clothing to accent your stay in Mexico Beach.</p>
<p>3102 Highway 98</p>
<p>Mexico Beach, FL</p>
<p>Phone: 850-648-4200</p>
```

Microdata formatted code for business details

```
<div itemscope
itemtype="http://schema.org/LocalBusiness">
  <h1><span itemprop="name">Beachwalk Beachwear &
Giftware</span></h1>
  <span itemprop="description"> A superb collection of
fine gifts and clothing
  to accent your stay in Mexico Beach.</span>
  <div itemprop="address" itemscope
itemtype="http://schema.org/PostalAddress">
   <span itemprop="streetAddress">3102 Highway
98</span>
   <span itemprop="addressLocality">Mexico
Beach</span>,
```

```
<span itemprop="addressRegion">FL</span>
</div>
 Phone: <span itemprop="telephone">850-648-
4200</span>
</div>
```

You can see how the above code gives the search engine a friendly nudge to recognize the information as a business listing, such as the address and the phone number.

While the above example will be just enough if you have a simple business listing, if you have any of the earlier-mentioned types of information on your site, you'll have to log on to schema.org to follow their documentation to ensure your data is correctly formatted.

Schema.org
http://schema.org

FACEBOOK OPEN GRAPH.

While we know schema.org is the best approach for adding meta data to your site, there is one additional meta data technology you should also use.

Facebook's Open Graph language allows you to determine how your site listing appears when shared on Facebook.

If you do not include Facebook's Open Graph code on your site, when a user shares your content on Facebook it will show a plain listing on the news feed, with the responsibility on the user to describe the article and make it worth reading. If you include Facebook Open Graph code, it comes up looking sexy, just like your search listings if you have been using your meta title and meta description tags correctly.

By putting your best foot forward, and making your listing show up correctly on Facebook, you will encourage more customers to click to your site, and increase the amount of likes and shares of your page. This will increase the social signals of the page.

Here's an example of properly formatted meta code using Facebook Open Graph. As you can see, there are only minor tweaks required to make your page show up nicely on Facebook's news feed. So go ahead and use it on your site!

```
<title>Buy Baseball Jackets Online</title>
<meta property='og:type' content='site'>
<meta property-'og:description' name='description'
content='Wide range of Baseball Jackets online, for all
leagues and players. Free delivery and free returns both-
ways in USA.'/>
```

If you're worried about confusing search engines by using several 'structured data' technologies at the same time, such as Open Graph and schema.org, don't worry, you won't have any problems.

Facebook Open Graph is mainly used by Facebook's web crawler, not by search engines, so you can use Open Graph and schema.org in tandem without any problems.

If you want to read up further on Facebook's Open Graph, or if you have complex types of listings on your site, checkout Facebook's Open Graph guide below.

Open Graph Protocol
http://ogp.me

POWERFUL SEO TOOLS.

There are many powerful SEO tools that can help save hours, days or even weeks of your time.

The following tools can help find link building opportunities, diagnose site issues, create easy-to-understand SEO reports, make Google crawl your site faster and much more. More often than not, the below tools will provide information you need to achieve high rankings, and reveal link building opportunities so you can go out and get those high rankings.

Are there more SEO tools out there than in this list? Sure. SEO tools are a dime a dozen. The following is a selection of the tools I have found useful over the years and the tools mentioned in this book for ease of reference. Some are free, some are paid, but most offer a free trial long enough to start optimizing your site. I have no affiliation with any of these sites, I've just listed tools that I find useful. So jump in and have fun.

RESEARCH TOOLS.

Google Adwords Keyword Planner
http://www.google.com/intl/en/adwords/

The Google Adwords Keyword Planner has been mentioned several times throughout this book for good reason, it allows you to download estimated traffic for keywords users are typing into Google's search box — powerful knowledge to have in your SEO toolkit. You can see how many times a keyword has been searched in Google, you can also narrow this down by country and even device type, including mobile phones and so on. During recent years, Google have clamped down on the free data available to non-paying users, to access all the research data you will need an active AdWords campaign and must be regularly spending at least a modest amount of money.

Google Trends -Free
http://www.google.com/trends/

Google Trends provides powerful stats of search trends over time. Great for seeing how your market performs overall, and how demand changes over time for your keywords.

Market Samurai - Free to start. $149 for pro users.
http://www.marketsamurai.com/

Market Samurai is one of those reliable tools that have been around in the SEO industry for many years.

The favorite keyword research tool of many SEO gurus, Market Samurai is powerful for generating ideas for keywords and analyzing keywords for competitiveness — so you can uncover keywords you can target for easy rankings.

Moz - Free and Paid.
http://moz.com/tools

No book on SEO would ever be complete without a
mention of Moz. Moz offers keyword analysis, brand
monitoring, rankings tracking, on-page SEO suggestions,
search engine crawl tests, and much more. An essential
toolbox for every SEO practitioner, from beginner to
advanced.

SEOBook Keyword Analyzer - Free
http://tools.seobook.com/general/keyword-density/

By simply entering the URL to any page on your site, you
can see a chart of the most optimized keywords on the
page. This is great for getting a visual indication of
keywords search engines are likely to pick up on the page.

SEOQuake - Free
http://www.seoquake.com/

The SEOQuake toolbar gives you a powerful set of stats
for any site you visit, right within your browser.

SEOQuake also has a great option that gives you the
important stats for pages ranking in Google's search
results. A great tool for snooping on competitors and
doing market research.

SEOQuake's powerful toolbar works on Google Chrome,
Safari & Firefox.

Ubersuggest - Free
http://ubersuggest.io/

Automatically download the auto-suggested keywords from Google's search results for a nice, juicy collection of long-tail keywords.

OPTIMIZATION TOOLS.

Google Page Speed Insights - Free
https://developers.google.com/speed/pagespeed/insight
s

Google Page Speed Insights is a fantastic tool provided by Google to help speed up your site. Google Page Speed Insights will give you a score on how well your load time is performing, and provide a simple set of suggestions to forward to your developers and speed up your site.

Google Snippet Optimization Tool - Free
http://www.seomofo.com/snippet-optimizer.html

This handy little tool lets you type out title tags and meta tags and see a live preview of how your site will appear in the search engines.

Google Search Console - Free
https://www.google.com/webmasters/tools/home?hl=e
n

Google Search Console is another great tool, and if you haven't got Google Search Console set up, drop what you are doing and set it up now!

Google Search Console will report urgent messages if there are any severe problems when Google comes along and crawls your site. You can also submit your sitemap directly to Google from within Google Search Console, meaning you know Google has been given a friendly nudge to come around and pick up all the content on your site. This is a must-have SEO tool for every site.

HTTP Status Code Checker
https://httpstatus.io/

If you have ever setup a URL redirect, or asked your developer to, it's always a good idea to check and ensure the redirect has been setup correctly.

Use the redirect checker to make sure your redirects are returning successful responses to the web browser, so you can feel confident Google is picking it up properly too.

Robots.txt Analyzer - Free
http://tools.seobook.com/robots-txt/analyzer/

Many robots.txt files can often have slight errors that are difficult to pick up, especially for larger sites. Run your robots.txt file through this tool for a free analysis to see if there are any errors.

Robots.txt Generator -Free
http://www.yellowpipe.com/yis/tools/robots.txt/

If you're lazy like I am, you'll love this free robots.txt generator. Works great for the most basic or advanced robots.txt users to create robots.txt files quickly and easily.

Schema Creator - Free
http://schema-creator.org/

Great and easy-to-use tool to automatically generate your schema.org markup.

SEO Browser - Free
http://seo-browser.com

Takes a webpage or site, and shows you what it looks like to a search engine, without graphics and layout. This is a fantastic tool for getting a bird's-eye view of what Google is going to pick up on your site.

Tools Pingdom - Free
http://tools.pingdom.com/fpt/

Pingdom search tools are a great to monitor how quickly your site is loading, and find opportunities to make it load even faster.

With the Pingdom Speed test you can see how fast your site loads, and how large the files are on your site. You can easily find the large files on your site that are chewing up resources and bloating your load time.

Pingdom also offers a really nifty service to monitor your site uptime, and send you a text message and email alert whenever your server experiences problems and goes down for whatever reason. You can find out before anybody else and jump on your web hosting provider and ask them to fix any problems, before you lose too much traffic!

Traffic Travis - Free for beginners. $97 once off for Pro users.
http://www.traffictravis.com

Traffic Travis is a great and simple SEO overview tool. Unlike many of the other tools listed, Traffic Travis is a downloadable tool you must download to your desktop (PCs only!).

Traffic Travis provides SEO health checks, competitor analysis, ranking tracking, linkbuilding research, and much more.

Xenu's Link Sleuth - Free
http://home.snafu.de/tilman/xenulink.html

Don't be put off by the old-school design on the page that offers this very powerful SEO-tool for free.

Xenu's Link Sleuth is one of the most powerful SEO-tools available, that will crawl your entire site, or a list of links, and offer very powerful and juicy stats for each of your pages, such as stats on which pages have 404 errors, 301 redirects, server errors, title tags, meta desc tags, the list goes on! This tool has been around for years, and is a must-have tool for the more advanced SEO practitioner.

XML Sitemaps - Free to trial. $19.99 for large sites. http://www.xml-sitemaps.com

XML Sitemaps is a fantastic tool for creating an XML sitemap to submit to Google. Useful for sites that do not have a built in XML sitemap functionality.

The tool automatically formats the sitemap so it is in the right format for Google and other search engines. With XML Sitemaps you can create a sitemap for your site within minutes.

LINK BUILDING TOOLS.

Authority Labs - Free to start. $99 per month for pro users. http://authoritylabs.com/tour/

Authority Labs is a great tool for tracking your rankings in search engines. You can also track competitors' rankings, too. Monitoring your rankings is a must for every SEO project, so you can measure improvements or trends over time.

Buzzstream - Free trial. $19 per month for regular use. http://www.buzzstream.com

Buzzstream helps you find broken linkbuilding opportunities and track your linkbuilding outreach efforts. Buzzstream will even find the contact details on the site for you. Can be used as an alternative to Ontolo.

Google Alerts - Free
http://www.google.com/alerts

Google Alerts is great for keeping an eye out for fresh new search results in Google.

You can put in any search term, add your email address, and Google Alerts will send you an email each time a new listing appears in Google's search results.

Great for monitoring new links pointing to your site, mentions of your brand, new content indexed by Google, or even brand mentions of your competitors — so you can reach out and build links or add comments.

Majestic SEO Site Explorer - Free to start. £29.99 for pro plan.
https://majestic.com

Majestic SEO Site Explorer is a lesser known, but powerful link analysis tool.

Majestic's Site Explorer allows you to download historical reports of links built to a site, so you can see the historic patterns behind a site's link building.

Majestic SEO also has a very powerful tool called the Keyword Checker. The Keyword Checker allows you to analyze the competition for specific keywords, so you can know how difficult it will be to rank high enough for particular keywords.

Ontolo - $47 per month.
http://www.ontolo.com

Ontolo is a goldmine for broken link building, making it very easy to filter through many broken link opportunities, so you can reach out and start building links.

Open Site Explorer - Free for limited access. $99 per month for pro users.
https://moz.com/researchtools/ose/

Open Site Explorer is a must for understanding the links pointing to your site and competitors' sites. Cheeky little tricks with Open Site Explorer include exporting your competitors' backlinks and looking over these links for opportunities to build links to your site.

BONUS CHAPTER: GOOGLE'S ALGORITHM UPDATES.

You need to be informed about Google's updates to ensure your site doesn't trigger Google's spam filters. In some cases, you can take advantage of updates to the algorithm and get higher rankings. In this chapter I will walk you through some of the major recent updates to be aware of. And at the end of this chapter, I will show you resources for catching wind of new updates as they are released. Let's get started.

HTTPS UPDATE & HTTPS UPGRADE CHECKLIST.

In an age of security scandals, mysterious hacking groups, Government surveillance programs — and celebrities sending nude selfies to each other — it's easy to understand why Google, Apple and other tech companies are encouraging everyone to be more secure. Part of this trend is Google's advocacy for website encryption. On August 26th, 2014, Google publicly confirmed they started using HTTPS as a ranking signal.

Since Google publicly acknowledged site encryption has become a positive ranking factor in its algorithm and also stated its intention to strengthen this factor in coming years, it's a good idea to consider securing your site with a security certificate as a standard practice.

If you're wondering what the hell I am talking about, you have probably seen website encryption in action when you log in to your Internet banking or Gmail account. When you see a green padlock at the start of the web address and it has HTTPS:// at the front, this means the connection is encrypted and the website owner has verified their ownership of the site and installed a security certificate.

Website encryption provides a direct connection between the user and the website server, a bit like a tunnel. Because it's encrypted if anybody tries to eavesdrop on this connection any information intercepted will look like gibberish. The only parties who can read the information are the web server and the user. Pretty neat, huh?

Unfortunately, installing a security certificate isn't enough to get an extra boost to your rankings. There is a migration process required to ensure Google picks up everything correctly.

I've outlined basic steps below for upgrading your website without any loss in rankings or SEO juice. But this process is substantially more technically involved than optimizing a few keywords on the page, you should read the supporting documentation by Google, ask your developer to do this, and maybe even consider using professional SEO help before completing this process.

1. Contact your web host or domain registration provider to install a security certificate. Common fees can range from $50 to $500 per year. depending on the type of certificate.

2. Make sure both HTTPS and HTTP versions of your site continue to run.

3. Upgrade all internal resources and internal links in your HTML code to use relative URLs. This includes references to HTML files, CSS files, Javascript files, images, and all other files referenced in your HTML code. This means instead of referring to internal resources in the website code with an absolute address (e.g. 'http://www.yourwebsite.com/logo.jpg'), it should use a relative address (e.g. './logo.jpg').

4. Update all of your canonical tags to point to the new HTTPS version of your site.

5. Upload 301 redirects for all HTTP URLs to point to the new HTTPS secured URLs.

6. Verify the new HTTPS version of your site in a new profile in Google Search Console.

7. Upload an XML sitemap to the new HTTPS Google Search Console profile. This sitemap should include all of the old HTTP pages from your site and the new HTTPS pages. We are submitting the old pages to encourage Google to crawl the old pages and register the redirects.

8. Update all links on your social media accounts and other marketing materials to point to the new URLs.

If you want a downloadable copy of this checklist, the SSL upgrade steps for SEO are covered in the free SEO checklist at the end of the book.

Before working through the SSL upgrade steps, make sure you or your developer read through the support guides by Google on performing this upgrade.

Securing your site with HTTPS – Google Search Console Help
https://support.google.com/webmasters/answer/607354 3?hl=en

Move a site with URL changes – Google Search Console Help
https://support.google.com/webmasters/answer/603304 9?hl=en&ref_topic=6033084&rd=1

DOORWAY PAGES.

In mid-March 2015, Google announced its intent to release an update targeting doorway pages in just a couple of weeks. Before I go into what doorway pages are, and how this update affects SEO practitioners, let's look at guidelines announced directly by Google on its webmaster blog. Its wording is somewhat vague, but don't be overwhelmed, I will explain how to avoid being affected in the following paragraphs.

Here are questions to ask of pages that could be seen as doorway pages:

- Is the purpose to optimize for search engines and funnel visitors into the actual usable or relevant portion of your site, or are they an integral part of your site's user experience?

- Are the pages intended to rank on generic terms yet the content presented on the page is very specific?

- Do the pages duplicate useful aggregations of items (locations, products, etc.) that already exist on the site for the purpose of capturing more search traffic?

- Are these pages made solely for drawing affiliate traffic and sending users along without creating unique value in content or functionality?

- Do these pages exist as an island? Are they difficult or impossible to navigate to and from other parts of your site? Are links to such pages from other pages within the site or network of sites created just for search engines?

From *An Update on Doorway Pages – Google Webmaster Central Blog*
http://googlewebmastercentral.blogspot.com/2015/03/an-update-on-doorway-pages.html

Doorway pages are low-quality pages created with the sole intention of increasing rankings then funneling users into hidden pages where the real content lives. It's an old school, black-hat technique sometimes effective for increasing traffic — until Google puts an end to it.

A red flag for this tactic is proactively building pages for search engines, but keeping these pages hidden from users on your front-facing website. Another red flag is advertising affiliate offers (a.k.a selling someone else's product for a commission) without creating real value or content for the user beforehand. Steer clear of these two red flags and you will be unaffected by the doorway pages update.

To be clear, if your site has a directory structure with multiple pages for cities or service areas, this is fine as long as the pages offer unique and valuable content for uses, such as; unique content, rich text and images, maps or videos.

MOBILE SEO UPDATE.

In early 2015, Google announced a game changing update for the SEO industry. As of April 21, 2015, sites with solid mobile support will rank higher in the Google search results for mobile users. Sites with no mobile support will generally rank lower in mobile search results.

Whether we like it or not, mobile users are here to stay. And whether we like it or not, Google is driving the mobile revolution. With the largest mobile app store in the world, the largest mobile operating system in the world, and the largest amount of mobile search users, I think it's safe to say mobile users are a priority for Google.

Google is rolling out this update to give webmasters a nudge to make the Internet more friendly for mobile users. If you are not supporting mobile users, it's time to seriously start thinking about increasing your mobile support, not just for better search engine results, but for better sales and conversions — a very large segment of your traffic are mobile users.

If you are concerned about your rankings for searches performed on desktop and laptop machines you have nothing to worry about. Google made it very clear this update only affects search results on mobile devices.

WHAT TO DO ABOUT THE MOBILE UPDATE.

If you want to increase your support for mobile devices and be more search engine friendly, you have three options:

1. Create a responsive site.

Responsive sites are the cream of the crop when it comes to sites that support both desktop and mobile devices. With responsive sites, both mobile and desktop users see the same pages and same content, and everything is automatically sized to fit the screen. It's also becoming more common for WordPress templates and new sites to feature a responsive layout.

2. Dynamically serve different content to mobile and desktop users.

You can ask your web developer to detect which devices are accessing your site and automatically deliver a different version of your site catered to the device. This is a more complicated setup, better suited for very large sites with thousands of pages, when a responsive approach is not possible.

3. Host your mobile content on a separate subdomain, e.g. m.yoursite.com

While Google have stated they support this implementation, I recommend against it. You need a lot of redirects in place, and must jump through giant hoops to ensure search engines are recognizing your special mobile subdomain as a copy of your main site. Responsive sites are popular for good reason: it's much easier and cheaper to maintain one site rather than additionally maintaining a mobile copy of your site on a mobile subdomain.

Google have stated that this mobile update is fairly straightforward, either your site supports mobile devices or it doesn't. Google will not reward sites with better mobile support with higher rankings over sites with average mobile support — for now. If your site supports mobile devices, you can rest assured you will most likely be fine with this update. Run your site through the below tool quickly and see if your site supports mobile devices in Google's eye

Mobile Friendly Test Tool
https://www.google.com/webmasters/tools/mobile-friendly/

The technical details of building a responsive site are beyond the scope of this book and could fill an entire book. That said, mobile SEO can be ridiculously simple.

If you have a responsive site that delivers the same content to mobile and desktop users, automatically resizes content to the screen, is fast and is user-friendly, all you have to do is follow the SEO recommendations in this book, and your mobile results will be top notch from an SEO perspective.

For guidelines direct from the horse's mouth, so to speak, you can read Google's mobile support documentation for webmasters and web developers.

Mobile Friendly Sites
https://developers.google.com/webmasters/mobile-sites/

Finding More Mobile Friendly Search Results
http://googlewebmastercentral.blogspot.com/2015/02/finding-more-mobile-friendly-search.html

GOOGLE PHANTOM II/QUALITY UPDATE.

At the beginning of May 2015, many webmasters and SEO professionals noticed a shakeup in the search results, which has been labeled the Phantom II update or Quality Update. What they saw was a noticeable drop-off, or increase, in large websites, of anywhere up to 10-20% in traffic.

While Google initially denied any changes, the SEO community dug around and confirmed the update with Google and that it affected large sites with significant page quality problems. Specifically, the update was a change to how Google assesses the quality of pages, and then subsequently lowers or increases their rankings accordingly.

If this sounds overwhelming, don't be worried — small businesses and blogs were largely unaffected. This website targeted large sites with significant amounts of user-generated content, aggregated content and aggressive advertising techniques. Examples include how-to type websites, large directories, click-bait type sites or social media sites.

Among sites negatively affected, there's a surprisingly small list of quality issues they have in common:

- Aggressive ads occupying the majority of screen real estate, above-the-fold.
- Duplicate content or pages, containing information lifted from other websites.
- Thin or light content, such as pages with only a few sentences.
- Poor quality content, such as pages littered with spelling mistakes and poor legibility.
- Pages with large amounts of low-quality, spammy user submitted comments.

With this update, we can see quality is continuing to be a high-priority for Google and we should be providing a high-quality user experience for all visitors. Provide legible, unique, and good-quality content, and you are unlikely to run afoul of a Google quality update.

PANDA 4.2 REFRESH.

Late July 2015, Google confirmed a Panda refresh slowly rolling out over several months. Wondering what Panda is? Panda is Google's spam detection technology that analyses the content, design, and code of web pages — everything that's on the page — to assess whether or not the website owner is using spammy tactics and trying to unfairly game the system.

Both the SEO community and Google were tight-lipped about Panda 4.2. This is due to Google's slow rollout of this change, Google released this update in increments spanning several months, making it extremely difficult to pick up exact changes to the algorithm.

Panda 4.2 is a refresh, not an update.

The exact terminology Google are using for Panda 4.2 is that it is a refresh, not an update. This means Google is only making small tweaks to the Panda part of the algorithm that picks up web pages with low-quality content. It also means sites previously hit with a Panda penalty will likely have the penalty lifted if they have removed the cause of the penalty (with typically thin or low-quality content being common causes of a Panda penalty).

Sites affected by Panda 4.2.

This refresh only affected about 2-3% of searches, only a fraction of sites compared to previous Panda updates.

If your site is a large directory, ecommerce retailer, publisher, affiliate site or blog affected around this time, it may be a good idea to look over your content quality and templates for any obvious Panda penalty triggers.

Examples include:

- Duplicate pages or content.
- Scraped content.
- Pages with thin or low-quality content.
- Aggressive ads above-the-fold or ads hidden in content.
- Aggressive popups or deceptive user redirects.

If you don't have any obvious content quality issues, it's likely you won't be affected by Panda 4.2. As mentioned, Panda 4.2 is a refresh, not an update, meaning only small changes will be witnessed, and you should only concern yourself with Panda 4.2 if you are guilty of any of the above techniques in your site.

GOOGLE'S RANKBRAIN & MACHINE LEARNING ANNOUNCEMENT.

In late October 2015, Google announced that its machine-learning artificial-intelligence technology titled RankBrain had been secretly influencing the search results. Does this mean sinister super-intelligent robots created by the genius minds at Google are slowly taking over our search results? Not really.

Over 15% of Google's daily searches have never been searched before. On these never-before-seen types of searches, Google don't have any historic user engagement data to ensure it is delivering the right answer. Understandably, Google needs a strong capability to understand the actual meaning behind a user's search query as they type it into the search box.

Enter RankBrain, RankBrain forms connections between clusters of words to get a better understanding of what a searcher really wants, even if the searcher only gives Google a small amount of information. It then delivers a relevant answer to the searchers query, even if the results with the best answers don't necessarily use the exact words as the user. RankBrain is also a machine learning technology, which means it progressively learns from analyzing old searches, so it gets better over time.

when was hillary's husband born

All   News   Images   Videos   Shopping   More ▾   Search tools

About 57,700,000 results (0.47 seconds)

Bill Clinton / Date of birth

August 19, 1946 (age 69 years)

 Hillary Clinton
Spouse
October 26, 1947

 George W. Bush
July 6, 1946

 Chelsea Clinton
Daughter
February 27, 1980

Feedback

In the above example, simply by searching "When was Hillary's husband born", the first search result lists Bill Clinton's birth date at the top of the search results. That's some solid guesswork from Google! We can see Google's strong capability at inferring the actual meaning behind our search, even though I only hinted at the person I am searching about. This is Google's RankBrain technology at work, forming connections behind the scenes. As popular trends come and go, presumably, this matching technology is automatically applied in new searches and organically changes to adapt with the times.

You may be wondering about the impact on professional SEO. The impact is very little. As yet, there have been no disadvantages or advantages reported by SEO professionals, except, it's as important as ever to ensure your page contains related keywords in addition to your targeted keywords. Always ensure Google has enough information as possible to understand the topic of your page, because now it's possible Google will deliver your page for even more search results.

While the implications on applied SEO is very little, if you want to read further the below articles cover this new technology in great detail.

What is Google RankBrain and Why Does it Matter?
http://www.forbes.com/sites/jaysondemers/2015/11/12/what-is-google-rankbrain-and-why-does-it-matter/

FAQ: All About The New Google RankBrain Algorithm
http://searchengineland.com/faq-all-about-the-new-google-rankbrain-algorithm-234440

HTTP/2—THE NEW TECHNOLOGY THAT CAN DOUBLE YOUR LOAD SPEED

The nice folk at Google, Facebook, Firefox and Chrome have been secretly working in an underground cave for several years, developing a secret technology that can almost half the loading times of most web pages. I'm joking about the cave but the technology is very real and now you can use it on your website too!

HTTP/2 is a new technology that significantly improves how servers communicate with web browsers, resulting in dramatic speed increases. And on February 11th, 2016 the Google Chrome Developers Blog announced the Chrome browser's exclusive support of this new technology, while deprecating a similar technology called SPDY. SPDY, the older technology for improving browsing speed, was originally created by Google, so for them to decommission SPDY in favor of HTTP/2 might give you an idea of what Google thinks about this new technology...it loves it!

If you are not familiar with it already, and if you are wondering what I am rattling on about, HTTP is the standard technology that all web servers use to govern how files are transmitted between web servers and web browsers. The old HTTP standard has been use in servers for well over a decade, but being quite old, it wasn't really designed with the high demands of modern web browsing behaviors. The way it sends files is a bit like doing your grocery shopping by purchasing one item individually, packing it in your car, and then returning to the store to purchase the next item, and continuing this way until finished. When you make a request to load a page from the server, your computer needs to open and close a new connection for each file needed to load the page, and can only have a maximum of 6 concurrent connections per web server.

Well HTTP/2 completely revolutionizes the way our computers communicate with servers. When your web browser contacts the server, the server returns a response containing all the files you need compressed into one neat little package. The end result is dramatically decreased loading times for all web users. Needless to say, with Google's strong ranking advantages associated with fast loading websites, this is a solid technique to have in your SEO toolbox.

Feeling skeptical? Check out the below resource comparing HTTP and HTTP/2 speed differences side-by-side. You might be surprised by the difference.

HTTP/2 Technology Demo.
http://www.http2demo.io/

While it is a great technology, there are a few caveats. Web browsers only widely support HTTP/2 on websites secured with encryption and security certificates, so you'll need one of those to get started.

HTTP/2 is supported by most browsers and web servers, but it is still largely experimental, which means it can be unpredictable, especially on complex websites. And it can be difficult to setup on your web server, it is something that should only be performed by a professional web developer or server administrator.

If you want to get started with HTTP/2, the best starting point is to contact your web developer and web hosting company to see if HTTP/2 is already supported on your server. Describing how to install HTTP/2 is well beyond the scope of this book, with the infinite amount of web server configurations often requiring different installation methods, but the below resources can be a good starting point for general information and technical information for enabling it on popular web servers.

HTTP/2 Frequently Asked Questions
https://http2.github.io/faq/

How to setup HTTP/2 support in Apache
http://www.rundef.com/setup-http2-support-in-apache

Moving to HTTP/2 with NGINX
https://www.nginx.com/blog/nginx-1-9-5/

ADWORDS SHAKE UP.... A.K.A. ADPOCALYPSE.

In late February 2016, many webmasters reported a significant change in Google's desktop search results. AdWords ads started disappearing from the right column next to the search results, and instead replaced with 4 ad positions at the top of the results and 3 ad units appearing at the bottom of the search results.

Google soon publicly confirmed on the 22nd of February, 2016 pay-per-click ads would no longer appear in an additional column to the right of the organic search results, with the exception of product listing ads for some searches. And for searches with a clear intent to purchase something, the results would show increased ad units at the top and bottom of the results.

No one knows exactly why Google rolled out this change, but it could boil down to a couple of reasons. An eye-tracking survey released in September 2014 by a firm called Mediative revealed that desktop users are primarily browsing the search results vertically, from top to bottom. Whereas previous eye-tracking surveys performed by the same firm in 2005 showed users browsing the results horizontally, from left to right, and then progressing down the page. Further, mobile users are only presented with vertical search results and ad units. It looks like a move by Google to shape the search results closer to actual user behavior, unify the results between desktop and mobile, and increase high-opportunity ad units for advertisers, effectively maximizing revenue for both advertisers and Google in one fell swoop.

Initially both SEO professionals and PPC advertisers were resistant to this change. SEO professionals were concerned organic results were being pushed further down the page while decreasing organic traffic levels. And PPC advertisers were concerned it would increase competition for ad placements while driving up ad costs. Actual impacts have been very little, with only minor impacts on ad costs and organic traffic being reported in the community.

Perhaps the most remarkable outcome from this update is Internet users' complete acceptance of additional pay-per-click ad units occupying a greater portion of the top of the search results, making it as important as ever for SEO professionals to ensure meta title and meta description tags are well crafted and click-worthy for potential visitors.

MOBILE UPDATE PART 2

On March 16th, 2016 Google announced new updates would be rolled out at the beginning of May 2016 that will increase the effect of the ranking signal that helps match mobile users with mobile friendly search results.

In the announcement Google states, "beginning in May, we'll start rolling out an update to mobile search results that increases the effect of the ranking signal to help our users find even more pages that are relevant and mobile-friendly." The announcement also states, "if you've already made your site mobile-friendly, you will not be impacted by this update."

On the 12th of May, 2016 this update was fully rolled out by Google, with websites fully supporting mobile being further pushed down in the results, while websites already having full mobile support being largely unaffected, if not receiving a boost from competitors falling by the wayside.

This update, and many others, is part of a long-term initiative from Google to encourage mobile support that has spanned several years. If you haven't already improved your mobile support, it's going to be increasingly difficult to market your website in the search engines. Read the mobile update advice earlier in this chapter on getting started, and you can also read the latest announcement by Google below, for finer details on this update.

Continuing to Make the Web More Mobile Friendly
https://webmasters.googleblog.com/2016/03/continuing-to-make-web-more-mobile.html

GOOGLE'S INTERSTITIAL UPDATE — A.K.A "DEATH TO MOBILE POPUPS."

Have you ever been waiting for a website to load on your phone, and found yourself waiting and waiting only to find a clunky advertisement popup and occupy the whole screen? Well soon enough this type of behaviour on websites will become ancient history as Google have plans to banish this type of advertising behaviour from the cosmos! In August, 2016 Google announced that coming the 10th of January, 2017 websites displaying obtrusive 'interstitials' to mobile users won't rank so highly in the search results. If you're wondering what 'interstitial' means, it's Silicon Valley tech-speak for a popup advertisement.

Let's have a quick read over the announcement from the team at Google and then take a look at what this update will mean for businesses:

"Here are some examples of techniques that make content less accessible to a user:

- Showing a popup that covers the main content, either immediately after the user navigates to a page from the search results, or while they are looking through the page.
- Displaying a standalone interstitial that the user has to dismiss before accessing the main content.
- Using a layout where the above-the-fold portion of the page appears similar to a standalone interstitial, but the original content has been inlined underneath the fold."

Examples of interstitials that make content less accessible

| An example of an intrusive popup | An example of an intrusive standalone interstitial | Another example of an intrusive standalone interstitial |

Examples of interstitials that would not be affected by the new signal, if used responsibly

| An example of an interstitial for cookie usage | An example of an interstitial for age verification | An example of a banner that uses a reasonable amount of screen space |

In other words, with the exception of cookie verifications and legal notices, age verifications, and app install banners, all other popups will lead to poor performance in the mobile search results.

I'm on the fence on this update, I know from experience a lot of website owners and business owners achieve a significant amount of sales from subscribers that sign up to their popups. Dictating the marketing of website owners to such a degree could be considered an over-reach from Google. By making it more difficult for site-owners to maximize the sales of their website visitors, are Google encouraging site owners to spend more money on AdWords and remarketing campaigns to encourage more customers to return to their site? I'll let you decide.

On the other hand, a significant amount of websites load unnecessarily slow and make mobile web browsing a clunky, slow and unreliable experience. Quite often, the cause of the slow loading is the site owner clogging up their website with complicated scripts and files that power the popup advertisements — sorry, I mean interstitials. Google have played a significant role in nudging website owners to update their technology and make browsing the web an effortless and reliable experience.

Whatever your feelings about this update, this is going to be a positive change for users and the way we browse the web on our phones will become faster and more reliable as a result. Just ensure you set a reminder in your calendar to disable mobile pop-ups before the 10th of January, 2017 or you will likely see some drop-offs in your mobile search visitors. Death to popups, long live browser notifications!

ACCELERATED MOBILE PAGES—A.K.A. MOBILE WEB BROWSING ON STEROIDS.

Have you ever asked yourself, 'what are Accelerated Mobile Pages all about, exactly?' If you haven't, then maybe you will soon, because the behemoth open source project known as 'Accelerated Mobile Pages' is about to get a major boost in the search engines. So much so, the Google team announced on the 12th of September, 2016 on the Google Webmaster Central Blog that 'later this year' sites equipped with the Accelerated Mobile Pages technology are going to be rewarded with 'expanded exposure'. The descriptions are noticeably vague, but before jumping to conclusions let's have a look at what Accelerated Mobile Pages are all about, exactly.

Accelerated Mobile Pages is a collaborative effort between Google, and a gazillion notable publishing companies around the globe, such as Mashable, The Guardian, The New York Times, and many others. The development teams of these organizations have been working together to craft a new technology making mobile web browsing faster, to a significant degree. To their credit, pages enabled with the Accelerated Mobile Pages technology are noticeably fast, snappy and responsive when you view them on your phone.

Specifically, Accelerated Mobile Pages is a framework, or a set of tools and guidelines, enabling web developers to build web pages that load blazingly fast. The core elements of AMP involve a specific approach to coding HTML, a JavaScript library that speeds up the delivery of files, and a caching network provided by Google that ensures speedier delivery of the files.

Some examples of techniques AMP employs to make mobile web browsing super-fast include:

1) Only allowing asynchronous scripts. Quite often websites won't load the page until particular scripts have been downloading in full, with this new restriction it will only accept scripts that load in the background and don't block the loading on the page.

2) Only running GPU-accelerated animations. Believe it or not, some webpages use unreasonably complicated scripts causing your mobile's processor to slow down, with this restriction the

AMP creators are forcing simpler calculations on websites that can be processed quickly by the graphics processor on your phone.

3) Pre-rendering, A.K.A Loading pages in advance. Another powerful technique, pre-rending intelligently loads pages you are likely to visit in the background, so that when you get around to visiting them there's no need to wait for it to download.

The above examples are only a few of the many techniques the authors of AMP use to make websites load significantly faster on mobile phones. In the end of the day, the proof is in the pudding, if you want to check out pages using this technology, the folks over at the AMP project have created a list of websites currently using AMP:

Websites Using AMP
https://www.ampproject.org/who/

Getting Started with AMP

While AMP provides a significant boost in speed and benefits for site owners and their users, to be honest, there is a solid amount of work required to enable it on your site. It's likely AMP may not even fit in with your current design or templates, requiring retooling your website layouts and elements to fit in with AMP's guidelines. The speed boosts are significant, however, so it may be worth considering implementing on your site.

Coding with AMP technology is well beyond the scope of this book, however, the folks over at Google and AMP have put together all-encompassing guides which are updated regularly, making it easier for yourself or your developer to put this technology to work. Have a browse or send the following resources to your developer, and you can get AMP technology running on your site.

Accelerated Mobile Pages Project – Project Overview
https://www.ampproject.org/
This home page provides a general overview of the AMP Project, written in a conversational style that should be understandable to both technical and non-technical readers alike.

Accelerated Mobile Pages - What Is Amp
https://www.ampproject.org/docs/get_started/about-amp.html
This technical guide provides a more detailed overview of the inner workings of the Accelerated Mobile Pages project, including tutorials on how to implement it on your website.

Accelerated Mobile Pages Project Github Repository
https://github.com/ampproject/amphtml
For super smart technical types, the AMP Project GitHub Repository has all of the updated files and resources needed to get your website running with AMP, as well as all of the source code which is open sourced so you can bask in its transparent wonderfulness.

GOOGLE'S POSSUM UPDATE.

On September 1st, 2016 webmasters reported seeing what looked like one of the biggest updates to Google's local search results in several years. With this being another 'tight-lipped' update from Google, webmasters were left to form their own conclusions about what changes were made. While online reports vary, three major changes are witnessed by most searches and consistent among reports:

- Businesses just on the outskirts of the city starting to rank higher for local searches.
- Multiple listings in the same category using the same address being hidden from the results.
- Physical location of searcher having a greater influence on the results.

The second update is the most notable. Businesses in the same category using the same business address are starting to be filtered from the results, with only the most notable business showing up in the results. This change could pose difficulties for businesses without a physical headquarters using a virtual address service.

These changes, while appearing to be minor, would likely require a significant amount of work and testing from Google's local search team, before being distributed to the public. The release of several changes at once might indicate these changes as an annual or bi-annual release of changes from their local search team.

Fortunately, the Google Possum update should only affect a fairly small subset of businesses. If you have a local business and you noticed any changes to traffic around the 1st of September, 2016 then the following article provides a comprehensive guide to this update.

Everything You Need to Know About The Possum Update
http://searchengineland.com/everything-need-know-googles-possum-algorithm-update-258900

PENGUIN 4.0—PENGUIN GOES REAL TIME.

On September 23rd, 2016 a representative from Google reported breaking news on their Google Webmaster Central Blog that the much anticipated Penguin 4.0 update had been released. If you're wondering what Penguin is, Penguin is Google's spam detection technology that assesses a website's off-site behaviour—backlinks in other words—and detects things high amounts of low quality links, suspicious amounts of anchor text using the same keyword, and other spammy practices related to how the website approaches getting links to their site.

At long last, Google completely overhauled their Penguin technology so it no longer functions like a filter that has been added as an afterthought, detecting and removing spammy websites from the results every few months or so. Google's Penguin technology is now a live part of the core algorithm, updating in almost real-time. To get a clearer idea of what the announcement entails, let's look at two major aspects of this update mentioned in the announcement:

- "Penguin is now real-time. Historically, the list of sites affected by Penguin was periodically refreshed at the same time. Once a webmaster considerably improved their site and its presence on the internet, many of Google's algorithms would take that into consideration very fast, but others, like Penguin, needed to be refreshed. With this change, Penguin's data is refreshed in real time, so changes will be visible much faster, typically taking effect shortly after we recrawl and reindex a page. It also means we're not going to comment on future refreshes."
- "Penguin is now more granular. Penguin now devalues spam by adjusting ranking based on spam signals, rather than affecting ranking of the whole site."

This update going real time is big news for webmasters. Previously, Penguin updates were released every few months and sometimes longer. As a result, webmasters getting penalized by the Penguin filter would get their whole website blacklisted from Google, and then would have to wait several months for Google to remove the penalty after rectifying the spammy behaviour. Now with Google's major spam technology updating in real-time, website owners who run afoul of Google's spam filtering can get themselves out of hot water much more quickly, while Google's search results will become even more relevant and up-to-date for users, so it's a win-win.

The other point the Google team noted in their announcement is the update has a more granular approach, now updating *rankings* based on spam signals, as opposed to devaluing whole sites. This is a reasonable update by Google, by focusing on penalizing particular rankings and pages, as opposed to whole sites, the outcome is a more fine-tuned set of search results. There will also be less backlash and negative fallout associated with unfortunate website owners having their whole website delisted. Another positive change for webmasters.

This is a fairly positive update overall for webmasters, but there is one aspect to the announcement that makes me a little concerned, 'It also means we're no longer going to comment on future refreshes.' In this comment, it does appear that Google are essentially giving themselves a hall pass from any further comments on their spam filtering technology. In other words, we're going to get much less specific information on link building strategies that Google considers 'spammy'.

If you have experienced any fluctuations in rankings surrounding this update, it would be prudent to have a look over your link building. The following areas are common red flags that could potentially trigger a Penguin penalty:

- Links from private blog networks or paid-link schemes.
- Spammy over-optimized anchor texts.
- Unnatural amounts of links acquired from similar sources.
- Large amounts of links from spammy websites.

- Lack of stop-words or branded keywords in the links pointing to your website.

Just don't throw the baby out with the bathwater and start overhauling your links unless you are completely confident you know what you are doing. The best approach is to keep a cool head, avoid using spammy link building techniques, and follow 'white hat' approaches to link building at all times.

GOOGLE FRED—DIAGNOSIS AND RECOVERY.

Around the 8th of March, 2017 murmurs of a Google update echoed around the blogosphere. Prominent Google staff member, Garry Illyes previously joked that all future updates should be named "Fred", so the SEO community obliged and labelled this newest update Fred. While many professionals initially debated the significance and exact focus of the update, industry stalwarts Barry Schwartz from Search Engine Land and Juan Goanzalez from Sistrix put their heads down and analyzed hundreds of sites that lost massive amounts of traffic, up to 90% of traffic in some cases, and they found something interesting.

Sites affected were guilty of a surprisingly small set of possible infringements, two in fact, which could be witnessed on affected sites.

Common Attributes of Google FRED Affected Sites.

1) Sites affected showed a strong commercial focus over providing real value for users. This means sites with large amounts of pages filled with low quality content in an effort to generate ad revenue.

2) Sites affected generally feature aggressive ad placements, taking up a large amount of screen real estate "above-the-fold" or hidden in the content in a way confuses users.

Google FRED Recovery Steps.

The update is clearly focused on content quality, much like previous Panda updates, thus the solution is fairly straight forward for victims of this update — improve your content and take it easy on the ads. In many cases, site owners hit by the update made a complete recovery simply by dialing down their ad placements above the fold. If you think you were hit by this update, take a look at the following recovery steps. As with all updates, you should only complete the following steps if you are confident you were definitely affected by the penalty.

1. Look over your rankings and traffic around the 8th of March, 2017. If you experienced a drop off in both rankings and traffic on this day, and the drop off is significant (i.e. it looks like your rankings and traffic fell off a cliff) then it's likely you've been hit by Google FRED.

2. Next look at your content and advertisement strategy on your site. Does your website create a lot of low quality articles to drive ad revenue, or does it feature aggressive ad placements to drive ad revenue? If you're guilty of either of these, and you saw the clear drop off in traffic then it's almost certain you've been hit by FRED.

3. If you're guilty of aggressive ad placement above the fold, you want to try modifying your ad placement strategy. This includes reducing your amount of above the fold ads, and also spacing out your ads so they are not deceptively mixed in with content.

4. If you're guilty of having large numbers of low quality pages, you either want to improve the content or take low quality pages down. Improving content is the better option, if you make a recovery you will recover more traffic than deleting offending pages.

5. When finished, update your sitemap and resubmit to Google in Google Search Console. This step will encourage Googlebot to visit your website and pick up the changes.

6. Monitor Google Analytics and any rankings tracking software you use. Rinse and repeat if necessary.

KEEPING UP TO DATE WITH GOOGLE'S UPDATES.

As of the last couple of years, Google updates have become progressively frequent. While I understand if the constant changes by Google make you feel like banging your head against the wall and doing a nudie run through the office, don't be disheartened. It can be easy to keep up and the below resources are great for staying updated. If there is a significant update to Google's algorithm, it will be covered on at least one of the following pages.

Google Algorithm Change History
https://moz.com/google-algorithm-change

Google Webmaster Central Blog
https://googlewebmastercentral.blogspot.com

Google PageRank & Algorithm Updates
https://www.seroundtable.com/category/google-updates

GOOGLE'S 2017 UPDATES—WHAT'S ON THE HORIZON?

You don't need a crystal ball or secret informer at Google to get a general sense of what may be on the horizon. After reviewing decades of updates made to Google's search algorithm, it's easy to get a general idea of what changes Google will likely make before rolling them out.

Before looking at what's coming up, let's look at what previous Google updates have in common. Almost all previous updates can give us insights into upcoming updates. Previous updates generally focus on two things; 1) filtering out spam and low quality websites, and 2) making the Internet and Google a better user experience. To figure out what Google may be working on, we should look at possible improvements with these qualities, and also updates that Google have publicly acknowledged as being on their agenda.

1. Security.

Google has already publicly admitted user privacy and security are becoming an increasing area of focus. After the HTTPS update rewarding websites secured with SSL certificates in 2014, it makes sense for Google to continue this trend and give more website owners a nudge to improve user security, perhaps further increasing the boost SSL-secured sites receive in search results.

2. Quality.

Penguin updates are generally those made by Google focused on link quality. Panda updates are typically focused on content quality. A solid update or refresh for each of these areas usually happens once or twice every year. It's likely Google will improve its accuracy in finding low-quality, non-relevant spammy type links, and further devalue their power. Google may also make a further Panda update devaluing websites with low-quality content, scraped content, or over aggressive ads.

3. Trust.

As more traditional businesses move online, leading to increased pressure on Google from commercial advertisers, we may begin to see fewer results for sites perceived as part of a bad neighborhood type network showing up in search. This includes sites advocating user privacy such as sites streaming illegal versions of TV shows and movies, sites with unethical or illegal content, and sites using shady marketing practices such as private blog networks. Authoritative brands with large social audiences and brand recognition may continue to be rewarded with higher positions.

4. Mobile.

Google started their pro-mobile initiative in 2015 and this is likely to continue, with mobile Internet usage surpassing desktop in 2016. Google's mobile index is separate to its desktop index, meaning mobile users see different results pages than desktop users. Now Google has specialized its focus on mobile users, the mobile results will be optimized and improved. Expect more impacts on sites that don't support mobile, or more sophisticated algorithms for assessing how mobile friendly a website really is.

An observation by Searchmetrics in their *2015 Ranking Factors Survey* provides a good insight into this trend and what we may expect to see from Google in future years, "Finally, links are becoming ever less important with the continuing proliferation of smartphones, as content that is consumed on the move is rarely linked rather shared with friends."

5. Search result layout changes.

Google continually makes small adjustments to how its search results appear to make Google more useful. Potential layout changes to results pages include better listings for mobile apps, more detailed listings for local businesses, and better support for listings using structured data markup such as schema.org. We may also see improvements to results for direct question type searches, such as FAQs and how-to type searches, as mobile users increase, Google will improve its support for mobile users needing information on-the-go.

That covers probable areas of focus for Google over the next 12 months, based on current online trends, and what many industry insiders believe are areas of focus for Google.

I am not a psychic and I cannot see into the future — the above are just educated guesses. Don't run out and change your whole business based on speculation. That said, keep these areas in the back of your mind, so you don't get caught with your pants down from a Google update.

Focus on improving the quality of your site, provide good mobile support, earn good quality backlinks, improve your security for users and earn social media comments and shares. If you focus on these areas it's unlikely you will run into any major problems, and you will increase your online performance at the same time.

BONUS CHAPTER: THE QUICK AND DIRTY GUIDE TO PAY-PER-CLICK ADVERTISING WITH GOOGLE ADWORDS.

WHY BOTHER WITH PAY-PER-CLICK ADVERTISING?

You would have to be as crazy as a box of weasels to pay each time someone visits your site with pay-per-click advertising, when you can rank high in Google for free, right?

Not necessarily, pay-per-click advertising has some advantages over SEO. With pay-per-click you can:

- Send customers to your site within hours, not the months it sometimes takes for solid SEO results.
- Track results down to the penny, and get very clear insights into the financial performance of your advertising. Simply set up conversion tracking with the instructions provided by Google, or whichever pay-per-click provider you choose.

- Achieve a much larger overall number of customers to your site by running pay-per-click in tandem with your other marketing efforts.
- In most cases, achieve a positive financial return on your marketing spend and keep on selling to these customers in the future.

There is one caveat to the last point. If you are a small fish trying to enter an extremely competitive market, such as house loans, insurance or international plane flights, it's likely the big players in the market are buying a large amount of advertising, forcing the average cost-per-click to astronomical prices, and making it difficult for new players to get a profitable return.

If you're selling pizza delivery in New York, pool cleaning in Los Angeles, or cheap baseball jackets... In other words, if you're selling a common local trade, service, or product online, it's likely you can receive a profitable return on your advertising spend.

While pay-per-click marketing really deserves its own book, this is a quick and dirty bonus chapter, jam-packed with just enough information to get a pay-per-click campaign setup, avoid common mistakes, and send more customers and sales to your business.

If you want to delve deeper into the science of pay-per-click advertising, I've included some great resources on AdWords at the end of the chapter.

Sound good? Let's get started.

WHICH IS THE BEST PPC PROVIDER TO START WITH?

There are many pay-per-click providers out there, Google AdWords and BingAds are just two.

Google AdWords is generally the best starting point. You can sell anything on Google AdWords if you have money to spend because the user base is so large.

If you're looking to jump into pay-per-click advertising, get started with Google AdWords. Move on to the other pay-per-click networks after you have some experience under your belt.

Here's why I think AdWords is usually the best choice for a first venture into pay-per-click advertising:

- Fast and instant results. Send new customers to your site within a couple of hours.
- Advanced targeting technology. Target users based on where they are located, or what browser or device they are using. Google's ad targeting technology is among the best in the world.
- With Google's search engine market share at 67%, and Bing at 18.7%, you can reach out to the largest potential amount of customers with Google.
- Due to the popularity of AdWords, there's a wealth of knowledge on running AdWords campaigns successfully.

ENSURING SUCCESS WITH RESEARCH AND A PLAN.

Like all marketing projects, for an AdWords campaign to be successful, you need to start with research and a solid plan. Without first defining your goals, and designing a robust strategy to achieve them, it's impossible to create a successful marketing campaign — you'll have no way of determining if the outcome is successful!

Here are some important questions to ask yourself before you get started:

- What is the objective of the campaign? Sales, web inquiries, sign-ups, or branding?
- What is the maximum monthly budget you can afford?
- What is the maximum cost-per-inquiry, or cost-per-sale you can afford? For example, if you are selling snow jackets at $100, and your profit margin is 20%, you really can't afford to spend much more than $20 on each customer you acquire. Write this figure down, and review it later. You may need to first run a small test campaign to determine if pay-per-click is profitable, and the right marketing channel for your business.
- What are the most common characteristics of your customers? For example, if you're selling late-night pizza delivery in New York, you don't want to be paying for the lovely folk in Idaho searching for late-night pizza delivery. Write down your customers' common characteristics, and later in the settings recommendations, if there's an option to target these customers, I'll tell you how to do it.

HOW TO CHOOSE THE RIGHT KIND OF KEYWORDS.

It's the moment you've been waiting for. The keywords! Precious keywords.

Just like SEO, getting your keywords right with AdWords is critical if you want a successful campaign.

Unlike SEO, with AdWords there are different types of keywords called keyword match-types. I've listed the main keyword match types below.

Broad match keywords.

The default type of keywords all AdWords campaign use — if you don't change any settings — are broad match keywords. With broad match keywords, Google will take any word out of your phrase, and serve up ads for searches hardly related to your phrase.

Needless to say, almost all new campaigns should NOT be using broad match keywords to start with. Have a look at the example below.

keyword:
tennis shoes

will trigger ads for:
designer shoes
dress shoes
basketball shoes
tennis bags
tennis equipment

Phrase match keywords.

Phrase match keywords will only show your ad for searches containing your core phrase. With phrase match keywords, you can exercise a higher level of control and purchase traffic from more relevant customers. And higher relevancy usually means more sales.

To enter a phrase match keyword, when adding keywords to your account, wrap the keywords with "" quotation marks and these keywords will become broad match keywords.

keyword:
"tennis shoes"

will trigger ads for:
tennis shoes
best tennis shoes
tennis shoes online

will not trigger ads for:
shoes tennis
tennis shoe
tennis sneakers
tennis players

Exact match keywords.

Exact match keywords will only trigger ads for the exact phrase you enter. Needless to say, with exact match keywords in your campaign, you can have a high level of accuracy, and achieve more sales. Exact match keywords are indispensable for every AdWords campaign.

To enter exact match keywords, wrap the keywords with [] brackets when adding keywords to your account, they will become exact match keywords.

keyword:
[tennis shoes]

will trigger ads for:
tennis shoes

will not match for:
tennis shoe
tennis shoes online
best tennis shoes

Broad match modified keywords.

Broad match modified keywords are a special keywords allowing you to have both accuracy and a large amount of exposure. With broad match modified keywords, you will trigger ads that include a combination of all of the words in your phrase.

To create broad match modified keywords, add a + sign to the keywords when adding them to your account.

keyword:

+tennis +shoes

will match for:
where to buy tennis shoes online
tennis shoes
buy shoes for tennis
buy tennis shoes

will not match for:
tennis joggers
buy tennis shoe
margaret thatcher

Negative keywords.

One of the most important, but easily overlooked keywords are negative keywords. Negative keywords will prevent your ads from showing for searches that include your negative keyword.

If you are using phrase match or any kind of broad match keyword, you should be using negative keywords. Negative keywords are vital for ensuring you are not paying for advertising for irrelevant searches.

Enter negative keywords in your campaign by adding a - minus sign in front of your keywords when adding keywords, or going to the shared library on the left hand column in your AdWords account, and you can apply negative keywords across your entire account, a great time-saving tip.

keywords:

+car +service
-guide
-manual

will trigger ads for:
car service los angeles
car service mechanic
car service tips

will not trigger ads for:
free car service guide
ford mustang 65 car service manual

When choosing keywords, you need a balance between keywords with a high level of accuracy, such as exact match keywords, and keywords with a larger amount of reach, such as phrase match or broad match modified keywords.

Use a mix of the above keywords in your campaign, then review the performance of different keyword types after your campaign has been running, when you have some data.

STRUCTURING YOUR CAMPAIGN WITH AD GROUPS.

AdWords offer an excellent way of organizing your keywords called ad groups.

If you organize your campaign correctly with ad groups, you can quickly see which areas of your campaign are profitable and not so profitable.

Let's say you have a Harley Davidson dealership, with a wide range of HD gear from bikes to accessories and clothing, below is an example of ad groups you might create.

- Harley Davidson motorbikes
- Harley Davidson parts
- Harley Davidson accessories
- Harley Davidson jackets

With ad groups you can:

- Create separate ads from the rest of your campaign. Great for testing.
- Have a select range of keywords, specific to the ad group.
- Set a specific bid for the ad group. Great if you have higher-priced products or services you're willing to pay more for.
- Get detailed data on the performance of your ad groups.

Structure your campaign with ad groups with a very clear and simple sense of organization when you setup your campaign. You'll get clearer performance insights, and it will make your life easier when you want to make improvements later on down the track.

HOW TO CRUSH THE COMPETITION WITH KILLER ADWORDS ADS.

Writing a killer AdWords ad is essential to the success of your campaign. Poorly written AdWords ads can increase the overall costs of your campaign, sending less traffic to your site for more money. We don't want that.

With your AdWords ads, you want to:

- Attract clicks from interested customers, not tire-kickers.
- Include keywords related to what the user searched for.
- Encourage a clear call to action and benefit for the user.

Injured in an Accident?
www.1800needhelp.com/
You May Be Entitled to $10,000 +
Free Case Evaluation. 24/7 Call Us

AdWords ads are made up of the following components:

1. Headline. Your headline has a maximum of 25 characters. With your headline, you should include the keyword the user is searching for, or capture the user's curiosity.

2. Description lines. You have two description lines at a maximum of 35 characters each. Your description lines should make it crystal clear what you are selling, the benefits of clicking through to your site and a call-to-action.

3. Display URL. You have 35 characters for a custom URL that will be displayed to users in the search results. Display URLs are great as you can actually display a different URL to the users than the URL of the page they will arrive on. You can take advantage of this to encourage more users to arrive on your site.

I've listed below some winning ads so we can see why they are so successful:

Logo Design ® *SALE* $49
www.logodesignguarantee.com/Logo-USA
100% Custom-Made Special USA Sale
100% Money Back. Order Online Now...

Injured in an Accident?
www.1800needhelp.com/
You May Be Entitled to $10,000 +
Free Case Evaluation. 24/7 Call Us

Flowers Online - $19.99
www.fromyouflowers.com/
Delivered Today Beautiful & Fresh!
"Best Value Flowers" - CBS News

In each of the above, we can see some similarities. Each ad has:

- An interesting headline. Each ad captures the curiosity of the user, through use of special characters, asking a question or posting a competitive offer right in the headline.

- Clear benefits. Each ad has a compelling offer in addition to the core product or service being sold, making the ad stand out from the search results, such as a no-risk, money-back guarantee, same-day delivery, or a free evaluation.
- A clear call-to-action. The first two ads make it clear what the next step should be. In the third ad, the call-to-action is not explicit, but it is obvious. By having "Online - $19.99" in the headline, and "Delivered Today", it is clear the user can order flowers online to be delivered the same-day.

If you want more examples of successful AdWords ads and why they crush the competition, the article below is a good starting point:

11 successful ads and why they crush the competition
http://blog.crazyegg.com/2012/03/26/successful-adwords-ads/

HOW MUCH TO PAY FOR KEYWORDS.

A common burning question for AdWords newbies is, how much should I bid on my keywords?

The Google AdWords cost-per-click network uses a bidding system, which means you are taking place in an auction with competing advertisers. By increasing bids, your ad position increases, leading to more traffic or customers to your site.

Here is where it gets interesting. Google awards an advantage to advertisers showing ads with high quality and high relevancy. This is Google's Quality Score technology. Ads with a higher amount of clicks and relevancy are awarded a higher Quality Score, and subsequently receive increased ad positions — at a cheaper price!

Keep this in mind when writing your ads and choosing your keywords. Your ads should be relevant to achieve the highest Quality Score possible, so you can receive the cheapest cost-per-click.

On the other hand, there is no clear answer for predicting your ideal bid price. You should only pay for what you can afford. You can find out how much you can afford by doing some simple math.

For example, let's take the below scenario:

- You're selling video courses for $100.
- For every 100 visitors, 3 turn into customers. This is a conversion rate of 3%.
- If you spend $100 on AdWords, and achieve a $1 cost-per-click, you'll receive $300 in sales, and $200 in profit.

Here's the catch:

You can only find out what your cost-per-click is after running your campaign for a while, when you have accumulated some reliable data. So run a small test campaign to begin with, to collect some data. Use the information to make projections, and only pay what you can afford in a larger campaign.

ADWORDS SETTINGS FOR GETTING STARTED.

The single most important factor to ensure your campaign is successful is to fill out all of the settings when you set up your campaign. Whatever you do, do not rush through the campaign settings, otherwise you will end up paying for advertising to people who have no interest in what you're selling.

I've listed recommended AdWords settings below for reference, but if you are not setting up your AdWords campaign right now, feel free to skip to the end of this chapter for closing recommendations on reviewing AdWords campaigns for long-term success.

1. If you haven't done so already, create an account at http://adwords.google.com. When signing up, enter your Google account, or let the tool create one for you if you don't already have one.

2. Once fully signed in, click on the big button "Create your first campaign".

3. Campaign name:
Enter a descriptive name for your campaign.

4. Type:
Choose "search network only" from the drop-down. This is important. Make sure you select this option, unless you know what you are doing, otherwise you will also end up buying advertising on less relevant sites.

Select "All features - All options for the Search Network, with Display Select". Why would we want to restrict ourselves and give ourselves less options and features? Choose it, features are awesome. Trust me.

5. Networks:
Unselect "include search partners". We want to advertise on Google, not other smaller, potentially less-relevant sites.

6. Locations:
If you are targeting customers from a specific area, country, state or city, enter the most relevant setting for your customers here. Whatever you do, don't forget about this setting, otherwise if you're a local business you'll end up buying advertising halfway around the world!

7. Bid strategy:
Choose "I'll manually set my bids for clicks". This allows you to make sure you are only setting cost-per-click bids you can afford. More on setting bids later.

8. Default bid:
Enter any number here, we are going to change it later.

9. Budget:
Enter your daily budget.

10. Ad Extensions:

Ad Extensions, otherwise known as sitelinks, are a great way to encourage more clicks to your site. Enter as many relevant entries as you can, if you have an office address and phone number, use it.

11. Schedule:

If you are only open during certain business hours, enter the hours you want to be running ads here. For some businesses, it's OK to run your campaign 24/7, because some customers will send an online inquiry if they arrive at your site outside of business hours. If you are selling something like a local food, such as a pizza shop, you might want to restrict your campaigns to only run during your opening hours.

12. Ad delivery:

Choose "Rotate indefinitely. Show lower performing ads more evenly with higher performing ads, and do not optimize".

Why would you want to choose this, you might wonder? You want to run your ads evenly, so you have reliable data when you review your ads, and can objectively see which ads are performing better for your goals.

You can leave the rest of settings for now, hit "save and continue", and you're good to go with setting up the rest of your campaign.

OPTIMIZATION TIPS FOR TWEAKING YOUR CAMPAIGN FOR BETTER PROFIT.

I've touched on a handful of secrets of successful pay-per-click campaigns, but I'm going to wrap up this special bonus chapter with the most important habit for pay-per-click success.

Review your campaign regularly.

Leaving an AdWords campaign running without keeping your head around the performance is like leaving a freight train running without a driver.

Regularly review your ad performance, ad group performance, keyword performance, and cost-per-click performance. This will allow you to back the winning horses of your campaign, and swiftly cut the losers.

Fortunately, the AdWords platform offers endless opportunities for deep insights into the performance of your campaign.

As a starting point, below are example areas in your campaign to regularly look over:

- Ad group performance. Review click-through-rates, cost-per-click, and cost-per-conversion. Allocate more funds from your campaign to winning ad groups, and decrease funds or pause losing ad groups if you see any obvious trends.

- Ad performance. Look for winning ads with higher click-through-rates, lower cost-per-clicks, and lower cost-per-conversion. Pause expensive ads, and create new ads to split-test based on your winners. Progressively build up new ads with higher click-through-rates into your campaign over time.

- Keyword performance. Review which keywords are running at a higher cost, which keywords have low quality scores, and see if you can pause any overly budget-draining keywords with low conversions.

That wraps up the special bonus chapter on AdWords.

If you want to delve deeper into the pay-per-click rabbit-hole, the below resources are a great starting point for anyone starting out with pay-per-click advertising:

Ultimate Guide to Google AdWords - Perry Marshall

The *Ultimate Guide to Google Adwords* by Perry Marshall is often the starting point for many professionals starting out with PPC. Offers a great overview of AdWords and delves into the inner game of successful AdWords campaigns. Great for beginners, but for more advanced techniques check out the following resources.

Advanced Google AdWords - Brad Geddes

If you want to be a pay-per-click guru, then look no further than this fantastic guide to advanced AdWords management, great for both agencies and business owners running their own campaigns. Brad Geddes' magnum opus on advanced AdWords pay-per-click advertising has been the secret treasure of many successful pay-per-click consultants, and is readily available in Amazon and many other book stores.

PPC Hero
http://www.ppchero.com

PPC Hero is loaded with free advice on the latest AdWords tricks and tips, but also covering fundamental pay-per-click methods that never change. Updated regularly.

Inside AdWords
http://adwords.blogspot.com

Google's official blog for AdWords. Great for the latest AdWords news direct from the horse's mouth.

That brings us to the end of the last bonus chapter of SEO 2017, and almost to the end of the book. Make sure you download the SEO checklist available on the following page as well as read through the final chapter for some closing thoughts.

BONUS: 50-POINT SEO CHECKLIST PDF DOWNLOAD INSTRUCTIONS

SEO CHECKLIST

SEO checklist for readers of SEO 2017 by Adam Clarke, available on Amazon.com

1. KEYWORD RESEARCH

Completed?

1.1 - Competitive research
Steal keywords from competitors using SEOBook Keyword Analyzer or SEMrush
Domain Analytics
Resource/s
http://tools.seobook.com/general/keyword-density/
http://semrush.com

1.2 - Brainstorm a master list of keywords
Brainstorm your own master list by sketching out a grid of words your target

DOWNLOAD THE FREE SEO CHECKLIST

We've created an extensive 50-point SEO checklist so you can more easily improve your visibility in search engines in step-by-step format, as a small thank you for reading this book. It covers the following areas:

- Keyword research and finding the right keywords for your site, which tools to use, where to start, and so on…
- On page optimization basics, optimizing keywords.
- Social media and web analytics setup tips.
- All technical areas covered in the book in an easy to understand step-by-step format, and much more…

WHERE TO ACCESS THE COMPLIMENTARY CHECKLIST

The SEO checklist is available at the following url.
http://www.simpleeffectiveness.com/seo-checklist

After downloading the checklist, make sure you remember to finish reading through the final chapter of the book.

FINAL THOUGHTS.

WE'VE COVERED A LOT OF GROUND

This book was written in a positive, light and conversational style in the hope of making a sometimes difficult topic readable for readers from all backgrounds. At the same time, if you've read all the way to the finish line you've covered a lot of ground, including:

- The basics of how Google works.
- Google's ranking factors.
- Keyword research.
- Improving your site's load speed.
- Optimizing keywords into your pages.
- Link building, examples of beginner and advanced strategies.
- Social media and SEO.
- Web analytics basics.
- Common SEO problems and solutions and troubleshooting.
- Local SEO essentials.
- Microdata and schema.org.
- Steps for securing your website with HTTPS encryption.
- Increasing support for mobile users
- Google updates, RankBrain, HTTP/2, Google's Interstitial update, Penguin 4.0, and several others

- Staying ahead of future updates.
- Basics for starting Google AdWords campaigns.
... and much more.

Congratulations on being a positive and proactive reader and finishing this book! The knowledge we've covered is more than enough to get started in SEO. It's also enough to increase rankings, traffic and sales if you already have moderate levels of success.

Don't forget why we learn SEO in the first place, details are important but don't get bogged down in them. I often see many readers get lost in articles, forums and blog posts on SEO and stop making progress with their projects or goals.

If there is one thing I want you to take away from this book, it isn't an appetite for details. I want readers to finish this book with a propensity to action. Of all the readers I encounter, the most successful are those with a positive and proactive attitude, those who put their new knowledge into action.

Remember, what matters most is you optimize your site well enough to beat competitors, make sales and grow your business. If your site shows stronger signals to Google than competitors, you will win in the rankings. Most importantly, have fun with it, make it your own, be positive and proactive!

~

WHICH WAS YOUR FAVORITE SECTION IN THIS BOOK?

Which one or two sections did you particularly enjoy in this book? Perhaps there's something you would like featured in the next update? I love getting suggestions, requests and ideas for improvement from readers. I want this book to be the best for all readers, which is why I use feedback in updates as much as possible. Even if you are unhappy for any reason, noticed a mistake, or want something included, give me a chance to fix it and email me at adamclarkeseobook@gmail.com. I'll be happy to hear from you!

WHAT TO DO NEXT AND HOW TO SUPPORT THIS BOOK

Reviews are vital for the support and success of self-published authors. If you would like me to write more books on growing your business in this simple and easy to understand format, please take a brief moment and support this book. Put up some stars, a review and any information on any areas you particularly enjoyed on Amazon. Let other readers know what is in store for them. Just a small moment of your time will sincerely make my day.

- Adam Clarke

http://bit.ly/seo-2017-book

Made in the USA
San Bernardino, CA
07 July 2017